To Sara

Into the
UNKNOWN

ANN M CONNELLY

Ann M Connelly

 FriesenPress

One Printers Way
Altona, MB R0G 0B0
Canada

www.friesenpress.com

Copyright © 2023 by Ann M Connelly
First Edition — 2023

All rights reserved.

No part of this publication may be reproduced in any form, or by any means, electronic or mechanical, including photocopying, recording, or any information browsing, storage, or retrieval system, without permission in writing from FriesenPress.

ISBN
978-1-03-915692-0 (Hardcover)
978-1-03-915691-3 (Paperback)
978-1-03-915693-7 (eBook)

1. Biography & Autobiography, Medical

Distributed to the trade by The Ingram Book Company

Table of Contents

Preface	1
Health Visitor Training 1974-75	3
Dalkeith	9
Newfoundland	20
Barbara	43
The Boss, and the Voice	54
The Convent	63
Mary Louise, Harriet and Jackie	72
Flying	85
University	90
Summer Work 1991	98
Thailand	107
Return to University	113
Quesnel	117
Victoria Again	135
Inter Tribal Health Authority	140
Summary	150

Preface

I worked as a public health nurse for thirty-five years: first in Scotland and then in many places in Canada. When it is known that I had been a nurse the inevitable first question asked is 'What hospital did you work in?' Public Health Nursing is a much different career than that often imagined by the public and a bit of a mystery. By telling some of my experiences I hope that the scope of the profession is given a new understanding.

My choice turned out to be the best decision I was to make regarding a career. It took me to many places and introduced me to a great variety of different cultures and ways of life. When asked — as a wee girl — what I wanted to be when I grew up, I replied, "A detective or an Apache." Becoming a public health nurse, in a way, satisfied these flights of my imagination.

I was lucky to find work in my field in many places where I could use ingenuity and imagination. The work in isolation, despite all the "heart in the mouth" situations, gave me a chance to use any ability I had to think of diverse ways of dealing with a vast variety of circumstances, including difficulties or problems. I was able to use any artistic ability I possessed, and it satisfied my curiosity, by finding out about how other people lived and worked in a variety of situations.

Into the Unknown

Detection is a primary requisite of any community health work and though, of course, I would never become an Apache, working for First Nations gave me some insight into their various ways of life.

Health Visitor Training 1974-75

I had been working in the Royal Edinburgh Psychiatric Hospital for four years. For the last two years, I had been the staff nurse in a ward where treatment consisted mainly of various types of group therapy. Everybody, both staff and patients, gathered twice a day to question each other and point out problem areas. This allowed the patients to consider various ideas and encourage self examination and development. Groups were mainly led by a psychiatrist, but everybody was encouraged to speak. We also participated in art therapy and on occasions took groups of patients on walks in the grounds of the hospital. Nurses did not wear uniforms in this progressive ward as they did in the rest of the hospital. The work was enjoyable, if challenging.

During that time, I was renting a room in a friend's apartment and was earning a good salary. Eventually, the thought of working in the community, where many of the psychiatric problems we saw originated, became a greater pull so I decided to further my studies, as a specialised certificate was required.

To get into Queen Margaret College in Edinburgh to certify as a Health Visitor, I needed to have six months studying midwifery. I had previously done two months in my registered nurse (RN) training, four years previously, and so applied for a further four months at the local midwifery hospital. This was a mainly theoretical course, with time spent on the wards observing in the labour rooms and caring for the patients in the pre and post natal wards. There, another five nurses — who had also hoped to get into college — and I made up the class.

We were regarded by the other staff as slightly inferior as we were never going to be "real" midwives. We mostly observed the mothers, the births and the routine of each department, but despite all of us in the class having many years of nursing behind us, even the blood pressure results we took were questioned. It was a tough time for all of us, but eventually it was over, and although at the time I felt it was a chore, I must have learned some things as it came in very handy a few years later. Plus, two of the nurses I came to know at that time became lifelong friends.

Going to college meant no salary, but I was very fortunate to get a sponsorship from the Lothian Health Board, as long as I agreed to spend three years working for them when I finished. This gave me a basic income with enough to pay my rent and food. In those days, health visitor training took a full year: from September to September. We were not given any summer holidays, but did have a week at Christmas and Easter. On my Easter break I took a trip to Russia. When I told to my class mates and the teachers of my plan, none of them believed me, as at that time Russia was not a place often visited. I came back with plenty of pictures to prove it had really happened. Each month, we had three weeks in the classroom and one week out with a field work teacher (FWT), who was a Health Visitor with extra training. Each FWT came into the college — on a rotation — to discuss particular topics. This allowed students to get a realistic idea of what the job entailed.

My first FWT was Marion, who worked in an area of Edinburgh called the Grass Market with another nurse. They had worked together for many years. Today, the area is gentrified and a sought-after place to live, but back then it was a pretty poor area with many problems. Marion was larger than life. She was physically a big woman and had a large personality. I enjoyed working with her as she seemed to know everybody, and everybody knew her. Street people, prostitutes, police, and the general inhabitants were all recognized and shown kindness. Often, as we walked the district, a window would be opened and someone would shout on us to come up to the tenement apartment to do an unscheduled home visit. We did hold regular baby and child developmental clinics, but our main job was in the community.

One of the places we visited regularly was a bath house. Here, there were two regular house baths installed. Showers were not very prevalent at that time in Scotland. A state enrolled nurse ran the baths, but everybody called her Sister, which then in Britain was the name given to a head nurse. She had worked there for several years and always wore her green uniform with an apron and nurse's cap. Like Marion, she seemed to know everybody. Some people came in to have a bath on their own, but often the police or a social worker brought them. Marion also, on occasion, escorted someone down on their luck.

Sister was marvellous with everybody. She treated all with dignity, and after they were cleaned up, she treated any lice she encountered, often by cutting the client's hair. While in the bath, clothes were washed and dried. If the clothes were in rags, second-hand clothes collected from various sources were given. Great discussions took place between Sister and the client about the best colour and style, if available, for the individual. People, who came in feeling terrible, often left with a spring in their step.

When the area started to be rebuilt and become more prosperous, the public health clinic where we worked and had been in the Grass Market for many, many years was suddenly deemed redundant. Marion and her co Health Visitor of many years were split up and transferred to a separate area of Edinburgh. Both the nurses found it a very difficult move as they had worked together for years and knew the area very well.

I naturally moved with Marion to the new clinic when I was on my community weeks. It was at the edge of a large housing estate where a great variety of families lived. It was very interesting to work in that neighbourhood, as the inhabitants of the housing estate were very diverse. In some cases, many large families lived in small apartments. In others, single people had their own places. Some people worked while others claimed unemployment benefits.

The area had a very bad reputation, as it was a large housing estate with several gangs. Nurses in general were well respected in these days, however, once you became known, you were often escorted from door to door by the appropriate "gang" member of that particular area. If anybody else came near us, they were told to get lost as this was their nurse.

Typical of large poor housing developments, many gang tags were sprayed on the walls, and other graffiti was evident. You never quite knew what would be found once the door was knocked upon, but everybody was visited who required a home visit, and a variety of situations were found behind each door.

I worked with Marion from September 1994 to May the following year, gradually being allowed to go out on my own in the district. This was great training, as she and I discussed what happened at the end of each day, Marion providing suggestions and help when needed.

* * *

In the summer months, all the students changed to another area of the city and a new FWT. This gave us an opportunity to experience a new area of the city with another nurse who might have other ideas on how the job should be done. Helen was a completely different kind of nurse than Marion. She was very prim and proper, always wore an immaculate uniform, and rarely sat down in homes. We went out on home visits together for a few weeks, but eventually I was on my own.

Some of my most memorable visits were to the King family. They lived in an apartment in a tower block. The new baby was on my list and I arranged to see her and the family at their home. I knocked on the door, which was opened by the dad. He told me to come in, but warned me to watch where I was walking. It soon became clear as to why, as there were no floorboards over most of the room. The baby carriage was sitting precariously on two joists. The floor had apparently been ripped up over the winter to burn in the open fire. To look at the baby, I had to walk along the joists to have a look. The parents did not find this unusual situation a problem and assured me that the bedroom still had a floor. I had to visit on several occasions and each time, acrobatics were needed. I have no idea what happened to that family. I had to report the dangerous situation, as one foot on the space between the joists would have resulted in landing in the apartment below.

At the beginning of September, we finally graduated with our Health Visitor certificate. We had a graduation ceremony at city hall. Despite the extra training, we were not given any more wages, but did get an extra week's holiday every year. It was good, however, to have regular hours and every weekend off. It was the start of a new phase in my working life, and I was excited to see where this new adventure led me.

Dalkeith

I started working in Dalkeith, a town near Edinburgh, immediately after finishing my training at Queen Margaret College and I had become a certified Health Visitor. By then, I was a Registered General Nurse, a Registered Mental Nurse, I had done a certificate in advanced psychiatric nursing and group dynamics, and I had six months experience in midwifery. Finally, I was ready to take on a new job in the community.

Dalkeith was some way from Edinburgh, where I lived, but by using the back roads through the countryside, it never felt too far. After two years of commuting, I finally found a tiny apartment in Musselburgh, on the coastal road just outside of Edinburgh. It was a bit nearer to my work. Buying this apartment meant that for the first time in my life, I owned a place and lived by myself. It was situated near the harbour, which I enjoyed walking to on my days off. It needed a lot of renovating, but with the help of my parents, it gradually became more comfortable.

During my second year working in Dalkeith, word came that Marion had died. She had apparently had a massive heart attack as she was leaving her office on a Friday night. The cleaner found her several hours later. I did not go to her funeral, as it took place during working hours and only one person from each office was given time off to attend.

Nonetheless, I learned that many, many ex-patients attended. I was so lucky to have met and worked with her as she was the kind of community nurse I admired. She embodied the best in health visiting, and by working with her and having the contrast with my other FWT, I saw the possibilities of getting work done through knowing the people and treating everybody with respect.

***

At Dalkeith Health Centre, I worked with two other Health Visitors. Jean and Leslie were both in their late fifties and had been in the job for a great many years. Jean was well known as she, at one time, had had a weekly spot on a local television program discussing health topics. She and I shared an office. The two women were wonderful to work with, and no matter how much training I had done at college, having mentors to discuss problems and the day's events with, made all the difference.

The health centre was probably ahead of its time, as many professions worked under the same roof. There were five general practitioners, three district nurses, a district midwife, two physiotherapists, a dentist, and the three of us health visitors. A psychiatrist came once a week and family planning came once a month. Several times a year, the whole staff got together for working lunches in the shared staff room. Here we hashed out new ideas and problems. The ability to refer and discuss patients at any time was a great benefit to staff and patients. Back then, in Scotland, every phone call made had to be paid for, and we were therefore discouraged from making calls. Home visits were encouraged, and we often did anything from a dozen to twenty each day. We worked from 8:30 a.m. to 5:00 p.m. every weekday, with a half hour off for lunch.

Health Visitors were paid on the last Friday of every month. The cheques would be sent to the nursing officer in a special pouch by a designated person, and she would bring it to us. On that day, the Health Visitors from the four small surrounding communities would meet at a local café for lunch. A baked potato filled with cheese and pickles was always my treat. Although we all worked in nearby communities, we rarely met, having very full days. As phone calls were discouraged, this once-a-month lunch was both a treat and a way of catching up.

***

Much of our work as Health Visitors was done on home visits, but we also organised and held clinics. Some of what we did included organizing and teaching prenatal classes. These were open to all pregnant mothers and did not cost anything. Every child at age eighteen months and then three years got a Denver developmental test, where we checked their hearing and eyesight and gave different dexterity tests to find out how they were progressing. In that way, we were able to pick up problems early.

Although we did not do immunizations — this job was done by a community doctor, who travelled from clinic to clinic — we organized the clinics each month. All high school students were given a TB test. This was always a huge undertaking where the Health Visitors worked together. I did not have a high school assigned to me, but became part of the testing team when necessary.

Another time we all worked together was to give all the children in primary schools a hair check for lice. We set aside a week in September and another in January to travel from school to school to provide this mandated activity. Now and again, we had to bring some children, with their parents' consent, to wash and comb their hair in the big tubs we had at the health centre.

Another job we were given was when a child had been admitted to hospital after a poisoning. We were informed and made a home visit to find out how it had happened. Back then, there were no child caps on medicine bottles, bleach, or cleaning containers, which was often the cause of the poisoning. We, by law, checked out every situation to give advice on preventing it from happening again.

A bereavement visit, where we visited all families six weeks after a death, was also part of our mandate. These visits were not always easy, but we went to make sure that the family was coping and that all monetary benefits were sent for and received. Often a family member was quite happy to have someone to talk to outside their circle.

I had two areas of the town to cover. My main area was Woodburn, which was a Council housing estate, mainly housing miners who worked at the surrounding mines and at the local colliery. I had approximately ten streets with about twenty family homes in each. Most homes were duplexes, but there were also a few with four apartments.

Each working day, rain or shine, I drove to one end of a street and walked along. I did not have a uniform, being in the first class of Health Visitors not to do so, but I did carry a nurse's bag. We had a fairly strict dress code, however, with a skirt being essential. Occasionally, in the winter months, our boss would phone to let us know that she thought we could now wear trousers, as it was becoming cold. Eventually, after many months, I got to know just about everybody. Families tended to live in the same area and often visited each other. This meant that I got to know aunts and uncles, grandparents, cousins, and other various family members of the babies, children, and parents that I mostly had as patients.

My other area of work was a good contrast to Woodburn and slightly out of the main town. Newbattle Abbey Crescent was filled with larger individual homes where mostly doctors, lawyers, and other professionals lived. Once a baby was on the way, and then born, it made no difference where they lived, as the number of home visits were the same for every family. Each baby got a visit once a week for the first four weeks and then once a month for the first six months.

Most people were pleased to see me, but now and again I was not allowed into a home. Sometimes they were busy, but on other occasions the reason was not given. With persistence, though, I usually got permission to enter. We made visits for all pre-natal patients who were referred by a doctor or the midwife. Once the baby was born we visited on a regular basis. As Health Visitors, we had no authority to remove children from homes. However, if we encountered a dangerous situation, we were obliged to report it to the social work department.

I once had a young, new mother to see and was determined, despite being barred by her several times, to get in and see her and the baby. On one occasion, the door opened slowly and a face peered around the half-opened door. Just as she was about to swear at me and tell me, yet again, that she did not want a home visit, a great gush of water rushed down the stairs. She lived on the top floor and the washing machine had suddenly broken, causing a torrent of water. I offered to help her clean up the mess, and she agreed. Together, we mopped and dried as best we could, which took quite some

Into the Unknown

time. My help with the mishap had broken her anxiety about having someone in her home, who she thought might criticize her mothering and housekeeping. As we worked together, she realized that I accepted how she lived. I asked at the end of it if I could come again the next day to see her and the baby, and she agreed. I saw her regularly after that, and in the end, she told me she looked forward to the visits.

I had a primary school in my area, which I visited once a week. During one of the visits, the head mistress asked to see me. Two children had been absent for over a week, and she wondered if I could do a home visit to find out what the problem was. I made my way to the home and knocked on the door. After a long time waiting, one of the children opened the door. He shouted to his mother, and eventually, I was allowed in.

I found the mother sitting in the living room right up against the electric fire, which was causing her legs to have what in Scotland is called "Tartan Leg," where the heat causes a pattern on the skin. She did not speak to me at first, but as I sat opposite her in silence she gradually looked up, and we smiled at each other. I noticed that she was bleeding down her legs and asked her about it. It turned out she was menstruating, but for some reason had not put on a pad. I helped her clean herself and with the help of the children, found a pad. I knew nothing about this woman, but after observing her, I realized that there was a psychiatric problem present. The children, however, appeared to be well, and they had food. We agreed that I should come again the next day.

In the meantime, I discussed the situation with the psychiatrist, and he agreed to see her if I could persuade her to come to the clinic. The next day, I drove to the house and was allowed in. The children were still not going to school. It later transpired that Janice, as part of her psychiatric problem, was paranoid and believed that the children were being harmed at the school. We got to know each other over time, and eventually, Janice was accepted into a psychiatric day program. While at the program, she met a man who had been bringing his mother in for care. A relationship developed, and many months later, they decided to get married. I was invited to the wedding, but had already made arrangements to go on a holiday, so I missed it. I did give them a wedding present, which was appreciated.

***

In Newbattle Abbey Crescent, the other area I worked in, one of the local doctor's wives was pregnant, and it turned out she was having twins. I did my routine visits, got to know her, and plans were made. Near the end of the pregnancy, a third heart beat was heard. It was quite a shock for everybody, especially the parents, as triplets are, then and now, a rare event. Three girls were duly born: two were identical and, interestingly, the third had different features. Over the months of visits, it became apparent that the single baby had a distinct personality of her own. Caring for a new baby is a huge amount of work for any mother, but with three mouths to feed and look after, it was a bit overwhelming. With the family's agreement and the help of the neighbours, a schedule was developed for at least the first few months. A rota was agreed on where the neighbours took turns to help with feeding, and others agreed to help with laundry. This worked well, and the family could not have been more grateful for the help.

On a separate occasion, the social work department phoned to ask me to visit a particular family as they thought it was needed. I duly went to the door and was told to get lost by the dad. As I left one of the children looked out the window, and I waved at him. For some reason, that broke a spell, and the door opened again, this time by the mother. I warily went into the living room to find three children, half dressed in a messy room, and the dad sitting with a very large Alsatian dog by the side of his chair. Both the dad and the dog appeared to glare at me. I asked if I could help, and the parents shrugged. We went over the kind of programs that were offered in the clinic, and with that, I left my card and the house. I phoned the social work department and told them that I had managed to get in and see the family and all three children. The person I spoke to was very surprised, as a social worker had been trying to get in for quite some time without progress. It emerged that neighbours had been complaining of shouting on many occasions and had phoned the department. Several tries were made and on one occasion empty milk bottles were thrown at the worker. I went on many occasions, sometime getting in and others not. I did feel threatened by the dog, as it always looked as if with one word from its master, it would have chased me out of the house. I wonder if my fear of dogs started then. Over time, I managed to go when needed, and although we did not become friendly, we at least managed to have a working relationship.

One of the new families in Woodburn was from Indian. I had never met anybody from India before, so was intrigued to meet them. I made my first visit and was greeted by the mum. The teenage son was severely handicapped and in a wheelchair. He and his mum were the only family I ever met, as everybody else worked. It was not possible to communicate much, even in broken English, but we smiled a lot, and I observed the home and the boy. I left notes for the other family members and somehow managed to let the mother know that I would come back the next day. A note was left for me by one of the other members of the family the following day, which started a regular written communication with them. In this way, I discovered what the boy's needs were and what the family required. Over time, and with consultation with other staff at the health centre, plans were made. I became a regular visitor to this family and soon enjoyed many treats of food shared with visitors, as I learned, in any Indian household. When I was leaving to go to Canada, I was given a small gold butterfly as a farewell gift, which I still have to this day.

* * *

A new policy was passed by the health authority which angered me as it affected some of my clients. As a teenager, I had been very active politically, going on protest marches against the nuclear bomb, walking in favour of nuclear disarmament, and participating in other causes I felt strongly about. Since attending these events was highly discouraged by our management, I wrote letters instead, to make my views known. A letter about the new health policy was duly sent to Margaret Thatcher's government. Instead of replying to me, the reply was sent to the health authority. They, in turn, informed my boss. She was furious and demanded that I go into headquarters to explain myself. At headquarters, I was asked into an office where I faced two very stern looking managers. They sat behind a desk, but I had to stand. A severe reprimand was given, and I was told that it would be noted in my record. At the end of the meeting, I returned to the car park to sit for a while in my car. It was winter, and there was plenty of snow on the ground. One of the managers came out to drive off. She spun her back tires and got stuck. I got out to help, and she just glared at me. Fortunately, I had some cardboard in my trunk and was able to push it in front of her back wheels. She drove off without thanks, but I never heard any more about the letter, and it was not recorded in my record.

I worked in Dalkeith for five years. For the first three, I worked with Jean and Leslie, and we had a great working relationship. They lived in a small town down the coast called Gullane, which was about a thirty-minute drive from Dalkeith. Every now and again, after work on a Thursday, we would all drive together to Gullane. I would leave my car at the health centre, as I stayed the night after supper. They both loved to play board games, and it became tradition to play after supper on these occasions. The year before Jean decided to retire, the New Year Honours list came out, and she was on the list. Great excitement was engendered not only in the clinic, but in the health board and the community. What to wear at Buckingham Palace became a frequent topic, especially the type of hat that was most suitable. Eventually, the time came for the royal visit and both Jean and Leslie travelled to London. Jean received an MBE from the Queen for her services to Health Visiting, and they both attended the garden party afterwards.

About a year after their trip to Buckingham Palace, both Jean and Leslie decided to retire at the same time, which was a blow for me. Once word went out about their retirement, many, many people came in daily to wish them both well. Several of us got together and planned a big farewell party, which we had in the local community centre. We had a sit-down meal, followed by speeches and finally, dancing. It was a happy, yet sad occasion. I went to visit them regularly, both when I still worked in Dalkeith and when I went home for holidays from Canada. They lived into their nineties, but died within a short time of each other, having lived and worked together for over fifty years.

Once Jean and Leslie retired, two newly qualified Health Visitors came to work at the health centre. They had very different ideas about how the job should be done. We managed to work things out, but I was very aware from the beginning that things would never be the same. After two years with the new staff, I decided I needed a change. About the same time, I saw an advert in a local paper for nurses in Canada with Grenfell Health in Newfoundland. I applied and was asked to travel to London for an interview. I travelled overnight by train and had my first experience sleeping in a bunk while travelling. The interview was interesting, as I had the impression that the interviewee did not know much about northern Newfoundland or Labrador, where I was to be posted. She certainly had never heard of the Eaton or Bay catalogue, as her suggestions for things I might need were interesting. I was offered the job and, since it was only for a year, accepted.

Newfoundland

Me dressed in my new winter coat and boots. Both were bought from the Eaton's catalogue after much deliberation. I was sure that the lady, who interviewed me in London, for the job, would have been surprised that such things were available.

Ann M Connelly

Early days

I arrived in Newfoundland on September 3, 1980, for a big adventure and an exciting change in my life, expecting to spend a year with Grenfell Health, who had recruited me. Friends in Scotland had begun to get married and have children, and with the changes in my place of work, I felt that I needed something new in my life. I told friends and relatives about my decision, resigned from my job, found someone to rent my apartment, said my goodbyes, and before I knew it, I was off.

My parents drove me to Glasgow airport where we said our goodbyes. I took my seat on a jumbo jet heading for Gander, Newfoundland. I surprised myself, despite being a seasoned traveller, by crying much of the way and have often wondered since if I had known somehow that I would never return to live in Scotland. It was a smooth flight, but when we reached the Newfoundland coast, it was foggy. We did manage to land in Gander, no doubt due to technology. Once I went through customs, I was informed that Grenfell Health had left instructions that the hospital plane could not come, and I was to make my way to the Holiday Inn, where I had been booked in for the night. The next morning, I packed, had breakfast, and waited for the Grenfell plane to pick me up. The fog, however, persisted for three days, during which time I explored Gander, tried a McDonald burger for the first time, and met another passenger who was also going to St. Anthony — on the Northern Peninsula — where I was going for orientation.

The fog finally lifted on day four, and we set off in a nine-seat plane, which was the smallest plane I had ever been in. Little did I know it was big compared to some that I would fly in. The husband of my new friend was the mechanic for the Grenfell plane, so I felt quite reassured that all would be well. We flew over vast areas of trees, many lakes, a mountain range, and saw very small coastal hamlets clinging to the coastline. I knew for sure that I was entering a world very different from the world I had known. It was exciting, but I also thought that I must be crazy.

My boss picked me up at the airport in St. Anthony. During that short trip, she informed me that she had just been given a promotion, and I was to take her place in St. Anthony. This turned out to be a stroke of luck, as Nain — on Labrador, where I was originally headed — had many problems and was extremely isolated. St. Anthony, at least, had a few stores, a hospital, and other staff. After I was given a couple of days over the weekend to acclimatize, I began to realize just how tiny and scattered the "town" of St. Anthony proved to be. The hospital, named after Wilfred Grenfell, dominated everything. He had been a missionary doctor from Britain who had worked in Labrador and northern Newfoundland earlier in the century. No longer a mission, there were still remnants of its existence with an orphanage, now apartments for staff, and a memorial.

I was driven to the furnished apartment I was to share with two other nurses. They were both Newfoundlanders and worked at the hospital. Being a nurse at the hospital included shifts, with night shifts a regular occurrence. As I was in public health, I had evenings and weekends off. This meant that I had to creep around, especially on my days off, in case someone was trying to sleep. I bought a radio and discovered the CBC which provided me with news and entertainment. We managed to co-exist amicably for just over a year, but never did become great friends. Occasionally, we ate together, however as they mostly ate at the hospital which was only possible for those who worked there, I mostly ate alone.

The public health office was a short walk from the apartment. At the office were three other nurses, including the boss, Joanne, and a secretary, Glo, who became a good friend. A public health doctor was based at the clinic and, although he had other duties, was available if problems arose. He made himself very accessible and like the boss, who had previously been the nurse in the area I was to take over, was a great resource.

In Scotland, giving immunizations was not part of our job. Therefore, I had to learn about the intricacies of administering the shots. I made sure that I did plenty of practicing on an orange, first, before seeing a baby. As there was a baby clinic on a regular basis in St. Anthony, I had plenty of practice with another nurse checking on me before I was let loose on the babies in my own area. Other than that, the work was basically like the one I had left in Scotland, with the exception of having a very large area to cover. I had eight small communities to visit on the coastal road, St.Lunaire, Griquet, Noddy Bay, Gunner's Cove, Hay Cove, Quirpon, Straitsview and L'Anse Aux Meadows, my furthest hamlet.

Before driving into my communities, I had to pass my Canadian driver's licence. I had been driving for years, and despite having to drive on the other side of the road in an automatic car, it was not much of a problem. The RCMP officer, who had taken me out, gave me a pass. He did not tell me, however, about passing the yellow school buses, which I had never seen before. This turned out to be a problem later, as I had no clue that passing the yellow bus when it was stopped was against the law. I was later given a reprimand when one of the bus drivers reported me.

Into the Unknown

* * *

My boss took me on my first visit to the district I would be serving a few days after I arrived in St. Anthony. She introduced me to some people in each community, including the principles of the four schools I had to serve. I had a Pentecostal high school and elementary school and a public elementary and high school. When needed, I helped out with baby clinic in St. Anthony, but otherwise was on the road.

It took some time to get to know the lay of the land, but people were very welcoming, and home visits were easy to make. Many nurses had worked there over the years, so people were used to having different professionals in their homes. There were no restaurants or cafés in the area, so at first I brought my own lunch and sat in the car to eat it, but it was not long before I ate with my patients daily. We shared whatever was available; often, I was given food I had never tried before and occasionally, food I had never even heard of. Cod tongues, turkey necks, baked squid, and seal were some of the things I was offered and tasted.

One of the other things I had to get used to were the mosquitoes. We had them in Scotland, as well as the famous midges, but they were nothing like the ones I now encountered, every day, when out and about. I had welts all over my face, and one day, they were so bad I could not open my eyes. Fortunately, this happened over a weekend and I could see again before I needed to get back to work.

It was not long — even prior to receiving my first paycheque — before I realized that I had a problem. A pain in my lower abdomen had developed, and very quickly I knew that I had a hernia. Moving out of my apartment in Musselburgh, and then preparing it for my renter with all the heavy lifting and the anxiety of the move, probably was the cause. I took myself to the hospital and was duly diagnosed. Since I was needed at my job, it did not take too long before arrangements were made, and I was admitted for a repair. I worked until Tuesday and was admitted to the hospital the following day. My pre-op was strong enough to practically knock me out. I nevertheless did have a general anesthetic and was kept overnight. The next day, the public health doctor and his wife came to visit, as did my boss and the lady I had met in Gander and sat with on the hospital plane to St. Anthony. I was discharged on the Thursday, the day after my operation. On the following Monday, I went to work slowly and slightly bent over. I was allowed to work in the main office in St. Anthony for the week, but went back to driving to my eight communities the following week. It took some time to heal, but I eventually went back to normal.

***

It was not long before winter arrived on the Northern Peninsula. I had driven in snow in Scotland, but had never experienced so much. Huge snow drifts appeared everywhere. I was very wary of driving and drove slowly, but with winter tires — also something new — I got used to it fairly quickly, as getting to the community was a necessity. Eventually, I learned to find out when the road was being graded and drove behind the grader for at least some of the way.

The main office had several vehicles assigned for use by nurses. I drove a small car, which suited me. We had to know how to change a flat tire and were shown how if we already did not have that knowledge. One of the other vehicles was an old army jeep. It would have been my transportation had

I not been too small — four feet nine inches — and unable to reach the pedals. One of the other nurses loved to drive in the jeep, and when we had to go together, we went in it. When it rained, all the files and anything else being transported had to be covered with plastic as the roof leaked.

On one of these trips together, we both got out of the jeep to attend to someone. As we left the vehicle, a boy with Down Syndrome jumped in and drove away. We ran after him, and eventually, he stopped and came out of the jeep laughing. It was definitely a lesson on not leaving a vehicle with the keys in the ignition.

In December that first year, my boss invited me to travel to Prince Edward Island (PEI) to visit her family and spend Christmas with them. We got a lift down the peninsula to Deer Lake where we caught a flight to Charlottetown. There, one of her family members picked us up. Once I was introduced to the family, we settled in. There was quite a bit of snow, but by then I was used to it. We had arrived the day before Christmas Eve, and after supper, we settled into playing cribbage, which I had never played previously. The next day, all the family arrived, and we spent the day decorating the tree and putting out gifts and decorations. As they were a Catholic family, they all went to midnight mass, and I naturally accompanied them.

This was a new and interesting experience for me. I had been to a mass before with a friend from student nurse days. However, on these occasions, I sat at the back and read a book. In Charlottetown, we walked to and from the church, and I experienced a very different Christmas service. Many people were greeted and the whole event took a long time. Once we got home, presents were opened with drinks enjoyed all around. Later that day, we had Christmas dinner, which was typically Canadian, including pumpkin pie. This was a very new experience for me as I had only seen pictures of pumpkins previously. Everybody kept telling me that I was in for a great treat because their mum was a great baker. I anticipated something very special as I was given a huge slice. I usually can eat most things, but had a very hard time getting the pie down. Fortunately, the family were busy and therefore did not see my reaction as I nibbled. That memory has put me off pumpkin pie, but interestingly not other pumpkin desserts.

On December 26, we went out for a walk in the snow, and one of the boys got frostbite on the top of his ears as he had forgotten to wear a hat. A couple of days later it was time to travel back to St. Anthony. We were lucky enough to find seats on the hospital plane once we got to Deer Lake, making the way home an easy and quick experience. This was my only trip to PEI and despite reading the *Anne of Green Gables* books when I was young — and seeing the television series — it was too cold and snowy to do any sightseeing at that time. I had to just imagine all the scenes.

The two girls I shared my apartment with had made arrangements to be with family during the holidays. One of my neighbours, a lady from Trinidad, invited me to spend New Year's Eve with her. I again experienced some food I had never tried before, which was much spicier than I was used to. She had invited some other single nurses, and we had a good time eating and drinking while watching her television.

On New Year's Day, some of us participated in the annual bird count, which was organized by the head of the hospital. We were put into teams and set out with our maps and species diagrams to help us identify the birds for the count. I don't remember how many we saw, but the number was recorded and added to the list.

Into the Unknown

After being outside in the cold for many hours, we were all very happy to go back to the head doctor's home where we were given hot drinks and an array of food. I participated in the bird count in subsequent years and enjoyed the camaraderie and the feast afterwards.

During the time that I worked in Newfoundland, I was sent to two conferences on behalf of the Nurses Union. One was to Winnipeg and the other to St. John's. I went to Winnipeg with the nurse from Trinidad, who was my neighbour in my first apartment, and another from Newfoundland. We were flown to Gander on the hospital plane, and from there, we flew on to Winnipeg. I remember very little about the conference, but I do remember taking notes as I had to recount what had happened — as well as any new ideas I had picked up — to other staff on return. We flew back to Gander where we were supposed to be picked up by the hospital plane. At the airport, we were informed that we had been dropped from the flight roster as there was a new doctor and his family arriving from Britain, and they had taken our place. This made us aware of the poor status of the nursing profession. We had to make a quick decision as the plane was not coming again for several days and we needed to get back to work. Two of us decided that the only way back to St. Anthony was to hitchhike. The other decided to wait for the bus, which came up the Peninsula sporadically. We set off, and within a short time, were picked up. Several vehicles along the way helped us get to Deer Lake within a reasonable time. From there, it became more difficult to find a ride as the hour was getting late and fewer vehicles were on the road. We had to wait at the side of the road for long periods, but eventually we managed — if exhausted — to get back to St. Anthony in the early hours of the morning.

My Clients

I got to know the clients in my district quite quickly as I visited each community on a regular basis. The majority of houses I went to were extremely well cared for, and it did not take long before I realized that although most families had little money, they took great pleasure in decorating their homes.

The majority of my clients were fishermen, with many supplementing their income with some sealing at that time. There was always plenty of fish and other seafood to eat, but rarely much money to buy a variety of other food. Additionally, as the landscape was very rocky, there was little opportunity to grow vegetables.

Though vegetables were not a constant in most households, bread was a staple. It was usually baked on a Monday morning, and a slice was a standard during meals. With a diet that consisted mostly of seafood and bread, however, diabetes was common and high blood pressure evident. Since much of the fish was kept for the winter in brine, salt intake was huge. As a result, I carried a BP cuff and a scale on each trip.

I decided that I should at least try and promote a healthier diet for the families I was visiting. To prove that it was possible my first task was to cut out sugar in my own coffee. In Scotland, I had always taken about two teaspoons in each mug. It took me a few weeks of slowly reducing my intake before I was able to drink the coffee without any sugar. I have never needed it since. I talked about my decision and how I had managed to cut out sugar in coffee. I am not sure if this stopped anybody else from consuming too much sugar, but at least we talked about it. The salt intake was more difficult to control. It was discussed when possible, but as fish had been kept in brine for generations, it was part of a way of life.

Squid, cod, smelts, shell fish and murre — a tiny sea bird — were plentiful at certain times of the year, and most days, I was given one variety or another for lunch. Some people were better cooks than others, but all were very generous and often put a special cloth at the place I was to sit at the table, to put my plate on, as I was a guest. Seal meat was frequently on the menu and being a very dark meat, it increased my iron intake over time.

In addition to eating copious amounts of seafood, I also tried my hand at fishing. I joined Glo and some of her relatives one Saturday to ice fish on one of the nearby lakes. We sat for a long time, fortunately in one of the huts many people set up yearly. Some fish were caught, but I can't remember catching any myself.

***

One of the homes I visited was owned by a couple who had fostered babies for many years. They had children of their own, but they were all married and away from home. Babies anywhere between a few weeks to a few months old arrived from all over the Northern Peninsula to be looked after until they either went to a family or returned to their mother. There was not always a baby in the home, but when there was, I was informed and did a weekly visit. I had to weigh babies by holding them up in a net that had a scale attached to it. I don't know how accurate it was, however, week after week, a change was recorded. It was always a pleasure to visit this home as it was obvious that the couple just loved babies and had great patience with them all.

Another client was very different. Billy lived by himself in a hut. He was considered a bit strange as he kept to himself and often shouted at children who got too close to his property. I was asked by the hospital to check on him, but told not to go to his place alone. One of the other nurses in the organization had previously visited him because he was ill, and I had her notes. I felt that I had no choice but to go see him, so I went late one morning when I knew there would be other people around. I rapped on the door, and eventually, it opened.

Billy was a man in his late sixties, a bit dishevelled with a scraggly beard. He did not look too clean. We talked about his health, and I was able to have a look at his hut, which was small, but did have a stove and a toilet. He didn't have a bath, so he had to wash in a tin tub, which I suspected he did not do too often. I ask if I could visit him when I was in his community, and he agreed. I got some funny looks from his neighbours when it was revealed that I was visiting. Eventually, we developed a working relationship, and I was able to sort out his needs and get some medications. I discovered that he once had a wife and child, but she had left him when the baby was very young, and he had not seen them since. Visits were uneventful on the whole, but occasionally I was surprised. Once, he insisted that I have tea and some of the bread he had baked. One look at the slice, and I realized that the black spots were not raisins, but flies. I drank the tea, but did not eat the bread. I am sure he ate it all. On another occasion, he showed me a wad of money he kept under the floorboards. I was shocked as he lived like a pauper. I was also a bit nervous as I thought that if he was ever broken into, I might be blamed for telling someone about the money. I am sure, however, that everybody, like me, could not imagine that he had any money.

People eventually ask me about how Billy was doing as they had noticed that he looked much cleaner and more subdued over the months. Finally, a family in the community invited him to dinner, and he went with a clean shirt and a jacket. Bit by bit, he was more accepted and, with my encouragement, was persuaded to spend some of his money to build a bigger place to live. The men in the community often built their own homes, and a gang got together to build his new home. Two rooms were built, with a separate toilet and bath. It was luxury compared to the place he had lived in for all those years. I visited him when needed, but he was often now seen out and about chatting to his neighbours.

In my furthest away community lived a very large girl and her father. I visited them on occasion, and on one of these visits, she told me that she thought that she might be pregnant. I was very surprised as she had to be well over 350 pounds, and had as far as I knew, never had a boyfriend. Dealing with someone so big and pregnant was definitely a problem, especially as she lived so far from the hospital. Once word went out, arrangements were made to have her taken to an appointment in a truck. At the hospital, she was weighed on an industrial scale and topped over 400 pounds. Apart from her enormous weight, she seemed to be quite healthy. My visits continued and arrangements were made — when her date was near — for her to be admitted to the hospital. It must have been quite a difficult birth, but she came home with a son. Many, many home visits were made in the beginning. She did somehow manage to breast feed and was a good mother. Since she was not able to get around much, either her dad or a neighbour took the baby out, although she was seen on occasion pushing the pram. I never did find out who the father was, or where he had come from, but I suspect he might have been one of the fishermen who came up from another community.

***

Religion was very important to the majority of the population in that part of Newfoundland. The Pentecostal Church members were probably in the majority, but there were also members of the Salvation Army, the United Church, and the Catholic Church. These Catholic families, who were all related, lived away from the other communities on one of the arms of the peninsula, which was isolated and a good kilometre walk from where I had to park the car. I did visit just to introduce myself, but eventually a new baby arrived, and I had to make several visits. In the summer, I had to go on foot carrying all my equipment. If I was able to let them know in advance that I was visiting, the dad would come and get me. In the summer, he came in his boat and in the winter, on his snowmobile. The whole family used to pile into the house where the baby lived, when I arrived. Grandparents, aunts, uncles, and cousins all came to see what the baby weighed, and a cheer went up when a correctly guessed number registered. I suspect they must have been betting on the result.

At one time, I had two dying patients in one of my communities who needed constant care. Their families looked after them full-time. As it became obvious that their time was getting near, I decided to stay in the community as much as I could. I had become friends with the secretary in our office and had stayed with her and her parents on several weekends. Their home was within walking distance of these particular patients, and I was able to sleep in that home and be called if needed.

One night, I was called to both homes. I had managed to put up an IV for one, but it became obvious that more help was needed. An ambulance was called, and in the middle of the night, the patient was taken to hospital. She unfortunately died about a day and a half later. The other patient died at home. I was called just as he was taking his last few breaths. I had become fond of both of them, so I was a bit stunned. I was even more taken aback when the family expected me to wash the body and put on his Sunday best clothes. With the help of a couple of male relatives, we managed to lift him into a coffin when it was brought in. I went to one funeral, but not the other. It was the only time I was in a Pentecostal Church.

Activities

I had worked in the St. Anthony district for nearly two years, having managed to renew my annual work permit. During that time, I realized that the children had very little to do there except go to school and church. Maybe this is why the pregnancy rate of teenagers was particularly high. I thought I might be able to start a group for girls to join. It would provide a meeting place where they could spend some free time and where they could learn new skills and enjoy friendship and collegiality. I felt that I should start with a girl's only group to see if it was popular. I discussed it with several people in the community — which had a small community centre — and a plan was developed to have a girls' club once a month.

Word went out into the community, and on the first evening of the club meeting, I arrived with Glo — my friend and the secretary of the public heath office — as my local helper. A few girls trickled in, and we discussed what kinds of things they would like to do. I had been in the Girl Guides for many years, becoming a Queen's Guide, and therefore had some idea of the types of activities that would be appropriate.

Over the months, the frequency with which the girls met eventually increased to every second week and many more girls joined. We started off slowly with some lively activities, like exercising and various ball games. In the summer, we were able to get outside and play team games. We also had wiener roasts, and in the fall, had a bonfire. One of the activities we had every meeting was a singsong at the end of the night. I remembered quite a few songs I had sung in guides, but had to quickly find others. As a family, my parents, brother, and I had all sung at home and in the car, and I was able to remember some of those songs. Others were found on television kids programs. The girls also often added to the list. The lack of internet back then made finding the words quite a chore, however.

Another activity that we engaged in was skittles, a game that is similar to five pin bowling. I made the pins using empty pop bottles that were filled with sand. We set up teams and had a league. It was great fun trying to knock over the targets, and everybody enjoyed seeing their teams on the roster.

We also started collecting the small baskets that fruit normally came in. With these, we made baskets for mothers and grandmothers for Easter. We made paper flowers and decorated the baskets. We sewed personal hankies and embroidered the initials of the women who would be receiving the gifts. A small amount of money was gathered by each girl every club night. This paid for the supplies and enabled us to put some chocolate Easter eggs into each basket. At an appropriate time, we set off to as many homes as possible and personally delivered each basket. The recipients were thrilled with their gifts.

It was not too long after starting the club that I was summoned by the Pentecostal pastor. I had met him on several occasions, especially at the schools run by the church. He was the father of fourteen children, and he and his wife were prominent members of the community. I arrived at his office on the day and time requested. There, he proceeded to ask me what we did at the club as he had heard various versions of our activities. After giving him an outline of our events, he proceeded to tell me that he thought I should not be continuing, as children were taught all they needed to know at church. I reminded him that all girls, no matter which church they belonged to, were welcome. I left the office with neither of us satisfied. It did not, however, stop my resolve to continue with the club.

After a few months, we decided to get matching T-shirts with the club name on them. Several possible outlets were found, colours agreed upon, and an order put in. Each girl had to pay for her own shirt, but some families donated money to ensure all girls had one. They eventually became a bit of a status symbol.

One day, I had the idea to put on a play and invite family. I thought it would be a good idea to make it a local story. I had never done anything like it before and decided not to mention my idea until I was sure I could pull it off. On my home visits, I had heard many tales of what it was like years before at school, and an idea developed to write the play around this topic. I talked to many older people about their experiences at school, and slowly, after many months, put a script together which eventually was called *Then and Now*. Once I put the idea to the girls in the club, many were quite enthusiastic.

We discussed who would play each part and how much work it involved. Individual parts were written, by hand, and girls agreed to memorize as much as possible. The idea was to portray a school as it was in the present, with a narrator telling the story of what it was like years before. We built a set out of found items and managed to get old clothes to kit out the girl who was playing the lead role of the grandmother. Others just wore what they normally had on at school. Great excitement was felt as the time came nearer for the production. We rehearsed regularly, which meant that I had to be in the community on many evenings. Finally, the big evening arrived. Nervous, we greeted many family members, who made up the audience. Some of the community members had volunteered to make tea and provide goodies after the performance and came in early to set up. The play went on with just a few glitches. These caused a few laughs, but mostly the audience was appreciative. Many were pleased to see their daughters on stage and gave us a long applause at the end. We all enjoyed the tea and goodies and the girls all beamed for a long time. I left the script when I left Newfoundland, so have no idea what happened to it. It was probably not the greatest writing, but it seemed right at the time and gave everybody something new to see and participate in.

Unfortunately, after I left the community, the girls club stopped. I tried to encourage my helper to continue, but she did not feel she was able to keep things going. It was a good idea at the time and well worth the effort.

Another activity I participated in was to go out as a mummer. This is a tradition in Newfoundland that is carried out near the New Year. I went down to one of the communities with Glo and her sister; we all dressed in borrowed attire and with our faces covered. I made sure that I did not wear anything that could be recognized. We chose houses that we knew were not particularly religious and where we would be accepted. We had to either sing, dance, or recite a poem to get food. This was reminiscent of what we had to do as kids in Scotland, at Halloween. I chose to dance, as I knew that as soon as I opened my mouth I would be recognized. Somehow, I managed some kind of jig. The two people I was with were recognized, but I never was, not in any of the homes. I can't remember if I managed to have any food that evening as I could not uncover my face.

***

At some point, the two girls I was sharing the apartment with decided to leave St. Anthony. One left to get married, and the other returned south to be nearer her family. I put in for a place of my own and was lucky to get a one-bedroom apartment in what used to be the orphanage. It was just across from the public health office. Another nurse — who had come from England with her partner, a dentist — decided to go home and I bought their television. An apartment of my own again and a television: I was definitely going up in the world. It was so good to have a place where I could finally relax, listen to the radio, or watch television — even if there was only one station — without worrying if I was wakening someone.

The apartment building, housed several health-care professionals. The physiotherapist for the hospital lived upstairs, and she played the guitar. A bunch of staff from the apartments got together in the physio's place on many, many occasions to enjoy an evening of singing. During that time, I learned many Newfoundland songs. We also shared food we each brought and had a few bottles of wine over the months. It was easy to just walk downstairs after a great night.

***

Another activity I tried was cross-country skiing after ordering my skis from a catalogue. Glo and I used to ski on the weekends. Often, when the wind was strong, we went onto the frozen bay, near St Lunaire, opened our arms and let the wind swish us along, near the shore line. Great fun was had without any effort.

Another activity was borrowing a snowmobile and taking it out into the bush. There were lots of pathways already beaten down, so we enjoyed going many kilometres. Occasionally, I borrowed a bike, and we would tour around, even if it meant riding on gravel. Once, I went out in a dory with some fishermen who were pulling in their nets. I don't know why I went, as I don't like being on the sea. There was a huge iceberg near to where the nets had been cast. As the fish were pulled in, the boat tipped toward the sea to allow the catch to be brought aboard. I was scared stiff and had visions of falling in and being crushed if the berg rolled over.

I had a few holidays with Glo over the years I was in St. Anthony. The first was to Nova Scotia. We drove in Glo's car down the peninsula and caught the ferry in Port Au Bas. We made our way to Halifax where we stayed with friends of Glo's sister. At that time, Prince Charles and Princess Diana were visiting after their marriage, and we joined the crowd. We explored the city for a couple of days and then set off to see the province. We found bed-and-breakfast places throughout and managed to cover many miles.

Disney World in Florida was another trip. Glo had never flown before, so it was quite an adventure for her. We flew to Toronto, where we were able to leave our heavy winter clothes with a relative of Glo's, and then on to Tampa. When the airplane doors opened, we were hit by very hot air, which we were certainly not used to, especially in April. From the airport, we hired a car and drove to St. Petersburg to spend a week by the ocean. We both got bad sunburns as we were not used to such intense heat. We headed to Orlando and on to Disney World where we were like kids, getting excited by looking at all the things we had seen on television. The Swiss Family Robinson tree house was my favourite. Epcot Center had fewer pavilions than it probably has now, but we visited all of them. We spent a day, before returning the car, visiting an elderly uncle of my mother's who had immigrated to America during the 1930s. He and his wife had retired to Florida from Chicago and lived on the coast, about a three-hour drive from Orlando.

Another trip I took with Glo was to Scotland. Before we made our final arrangements, however, my mother informed me that she and dad were going to Yugoslavia during that time. (This was before the war and the breakup of the country.) In the end, we all went together. We spent one week in the northern part of the country, in the mountains, and then moved south to the beach. While in the north, Glo and I took a bus to Venice for the day. This took a few hours, but was an interesting experience. After our first week, all four of us took a bus down the coast to a hotel on the beach where we were quick to find that nude swimming and topless sunbathing were acceptable. During our stay, we took a ferry over to Dubrovnik, which we explored all day. We saw the historic city before it was greatly destroyed once the war started. After two weeks we returned to Scotland where we were driven around by my parents. They took us to many tourist highlights for Glo's benefit. Among those places were Edinburgh and Loch Lomond. I also managed to visit relatives and friends.

Ann M Connelly

***

Prior to going to a work conference in St. John's, I had applied for another work permit. After quite some time, I had official word that my application had been denied. I wrote to the Liberal Party, who was in power at that time, enclosing many signatures of clients who had signed a petition started by a group in the community on my behalf. This was to no avail, and I knew then that my time in Canada was coming to an end. I learned later that all nurses from different counties were also denied new work permits as it was hoped that Newfoundlanders and other Canadian nurses would take these jobs. At that particular time, there was a glut of nurses in Canada.

I went to the conference in St John's with one other nurse. This time we were flown there and back without the difficulties encountered on my first visit to a conference. There were many booths with displays along the walls of the conference centre. The federal government had a booth and representatives from the Northwest Territories (NWT) were there. I got talking to a nursing officer from Yellowknife and told her that I had had my work permit denied, but thought that I would like to stay on in Canada for another year. She told me that the federal government was always looking for experienced nurses, and I should apply to them.

I applied to the federal government and was prepared to go to any place they sent me. I waited and waited, but did not hear anything before I went on a trip to Ontario to meet a friend of mine. She was coming from New Zealand to visit her brother. We stayed with her brother and his family for a few days, but the heat and humidity was more than either of us was used to. We decided to hire a car, borrow a tent, and get out of Toronto to cooler places. While on that trip, I kept phoning Ottawa to find out what was happening about the job. Eventually, I had the good news that my papers had arrived and been vetted. I had a new job in NWT.

I enjoyed the rest of my holiday, flew back to St. Anthony, and prepared to move. Saying goodbye was not easy as I had become fond of many of my clients. Many of them had become friends, who I had spent time with, on and off duty. I made sure that I visited as many people as possible to say a personal goodbye. At the girls club I did not have a going away party, but was given several small gifts. We had tea and cake at the public health office and I was given a wall hanging.

Barbara

I travelled from St Anthony to Gander in the Grenfell plane. From there I flew to Edmonton to spend two days on a tuberculosis course. In most of my communities in Newfoundland there had been TB, but now working for the federal government, compulsory training was expected. The BCG prophylactic test was obligatory for all babies in the NWT. It had not been given in other parts of Canada for some time, and was quite a difficult test to give. TB was also rife in the adult population, so the nurses working there needed to pay special attention to the issue and have the appropriate knowledge. Little did I know that this would be a fraction of the new skills I would have to learn quickly, and then practise, over the next few years.

In Yellowknife, I was picked up at the airport, and with the case I had brought to carry my clothes and personal items, I was taken to the regional office. At the office, I was only given two instructions: there was a Hudson Bay store up the street — where I could pick up groceries and anything else I thought I might need — and make sure I was back in an hour.

I rushed back to the office with my bag of groceries, where I was told that Joe would be driving me to my post. He put the groceries and my luggage into the van, and we set off. Joe was from the Dogrib First Nation and lived in Rae. As a child, I had played Cowboys and Indians and I'd seen movies, but had never met or seen a "real Indian." Joe had long hair and wore a bandana to keep it off his face. I had visions of an Apache. We smiled a lot, but said little.

The road as far as the airport on the outskirt of the city was smooth, but from then on we bumped onto a gravel curved road. I had no idea where I was going with this stranger. On and on we drove by stunted trees, lakes, rocks, and what seemed like nothingness. Finally, after 102 kilometers we came to a junction. One road went to Rae where I was to work and straight on took us to Edzo, a further 10 kilometers, where I was to live. I was both anxious and intrigued by the journey, but most of all I had no idea how to react to this person whom I had just met, and whose general image I had only seen previously on the big screen.

In Rae, where most of the population of about 1,000 lived, there was a clinic, a store, an elementary school, an RCMP detachment and as most of the population was catholic a Catholic Church and convent. In Edzo, there was a high school, an eight-bed cottage hospital (run by nurses), housing for nurses and teachers, and homes for several Indigenous people who worked in the school and the hospital.

During my first week, I lived with one of the nurses who worked at the cottage hospital. At the end of the week, I was informed that I would be moving to another house to live with the new nurse, who was arriving the following week. During the conversation, it was revealed that the nurse was a nun.

I had been brought up to believe that Catholicism was somehow suspect. Over the years, I had met many Catholic people and had friends of that religion. Still, a nun was a different matter, and I certainly did not know what to expect. I waited in anticipation, conjuring up all kinds of images.

Finally, the day arrived, and out of the van stepped Sister Barbara in jeans, a sweatshirt, and a parka.

We were ushered into our new home where Barbara immediately complained about the cleanliness of the place and the shabbiness of the bed linen and furniture. It turned out that the previous occupant had had a couple of dogs. It was obvious that she had allowed them the run of the house. The head nurse reassured us that the complaints would be rectified as soon as possible. I knew then that being a nun in this community had its advantages as the place had a good cleaning and our linen was indeed renewed.

The side of our house in Edzo. Prominent is the oil tank, which was filled when needed and was part of our rent. Keeping the house warm in winter took a lot of oil and we needed refills frequently.

Here I was, in a new place, working in a First Nation community and living with a nun. It was quite the contrast to my life in Newfoundland. There, the dominant religion was Pentecostalism, and most of my clients were fishermen. In my new surroundings the majority of the population were Catholic. People did a variety of work, however many had trap lines and went out to hunt regularly. Both my communities in Newfoundland and Rae-Edzo were very isolated and somewhat bleak with few services. This was quite a contrast to Edinburgh, with all its amenities, art, theatre, and museums.

Living in a house with a nun took me some time to get used to, especially when I had never met one before and had been brought up to think of them as something not quite real. Still, I had no choice as to whom I shared with, and we agreed to disagree about many things. No statues or crosses in the living area, time for quiet in the morning, and consideration for each other's space were the first rules we imposed. Gradually, we adapted and became firm friends, although we argued about many things, religion included. During our first summer together, a sister from Barbara's order came for a visit and to meet me. I must have been deemed a suitable companion as Barbara was allowed to continue working in the community without other sisters from her order being present. We worked in different areas: she in the cottage hospital and me based in the next village and flying regularly to three remote Dogrib speaking communities, then called, Lac La Marte, Rae Lake and Snare Lake, all north of Rae- Edzo. This gave us plenty of time for ourselves and allowed us to enjoy each other's company when we were home together. Over time, I discovered that Barb liked to clean, which was something I quickly appreciated. She was able to eat at the hospital when on shift, but I took over the cooking at home. We tried to eat together at some point over the weekend, but if that didn't work out, I would leave a plate for her to heat up when needed. She would let me know when the cook at the hospital had made cinnamon buns, and if I was able, I would dash over to get one. She would also let me know when she was doing a particular procedure, and I would go over and watch. This was how I learned to stitch up wounds and perform other nursing activities that I would need in the communities I was visiting.

Barbara liked to go to church not only on a Sunday, but on any occasion she could find. Neither of us had a car to begin with, and the church was in Rae. By word of mouth, people in the village offered to take her when they were going. The priest came to the hospital to give communion if there was anybody there who asked for it. Barbara, therefore, was also able to have it there. If no one was admitted and Barbara had a day off, the priest came to the house. I either went for a walk or, if the weather was bad, went into my bedroom when communion was being given. Father was Swiss, but had been in the community for many years. He spoke Dogrib, the local language fluently. Once we got to know him, he would sometimes come to the house to cook fondue for us. We not only had bread to dip, but plenty of caribou.

One Christmas, we decided to get a tree for the house. We went out with an axe to cut one down. We spied the one we wanted, but it was so cold that when the tree was being cut, many of the branches on one side fell off. We took it home nevertheless and had to prop it up on the table, against the wall, then secured it with string. Somehow, it became known that we had an interesting tree, and people came to the house to see it.

***

In Rae, there was a convent where three Grey Nuns (the Sisters of Charity of Montreal) lived. They were from Quebec and were French speaking. Two worked in the community for the church, and with the many catholic families to minister to, they were busy. Another, Sister Louise, was a nurse, and we worked together for a short time. Once she heard that we were to get a new boss and who she was, however, she asked for a transfer. I should have been alarmed by this, but as I had just arrived, I had to give it a chance.

If Barbara found a lift on a Sunday to attend church in Rae, I often went with her. I went to the convent where I spent time finishing the food preparation. This allowed the sisters to go to Mass, then return and eat. The dishes were often started, by the sisters, but I continued and either cooked or put any previously prepared food in the oven. We all enjoyed good food together, and then, one of the sisters drove us back to Edzo. A few times, when the lake was frozen enough and the day was slightly warmer, Barb and I skied over to Rae. It was a long, hard, exhausting journey, but at least at the end we were able get warm, have some food, and get a lift home.

* * *

I had annual work permits while working in Newfoundland been but once I had a job with the federal government, I needed to become a landed immigrant. The paperwork was done quickly and I went home to Scotland for my first and only Christmas there since living in Canada, in order to have my interview. I had my interview in Glasgow but it did not take long for the documents to be approved, and I flew back to the North West Territories (NWT) three weeks later.

While I was gone, Barbara had been given permission to get a car, and she and the priest had gone to Yellowknife to pick one up. What a difference that made. She was able to get to church as often as work allowed. We also went to Rae for supper at the convent now and again and shopped at the Bay Store, which carried most things. Until then, I had been getting the things we needed during my lunch break and lugging them home. On occasion, we would travel to Yellowknife to visit the sisters who lived in the convent there. We would also drive there on a rare occasion to treat ourselves to a Chinese meal.

Our road in Edzo where all the small houses were similar. The houses mostly housed nurses, teachers and the local staff who worked in the school and the cottage hospital.

* * *

Into the Unknown

The Pope came to the NWT on two occasions. Nurses from all over the NWT were flown to Fort Simpson for a week the first time, as the population would be increasing drastically over the week of events. Hundreds of people from all over arrived during the days prior to the big event including many families. They brought their own tents which were set up in a large field. Some nurses worked at the various first aid stations placed throughout the site. Barbara and I were designated to work in the hospital: she on day shifts and me on nights. I was billeted for the first few days at the home of an RCMP officer and his family, and Barbara had a room at a building designated to house health-care workers. At my billet, I had to share a bed with another nurse whom I had never met. She was on day shift and therefore got out of bed before I went in. One of RCMP officers was her boyfriend, which meant that I would arrive in the morning, exhausted from a night shift, to find no sheets on the bed. This happened on several occasions, and I eventually had enough. I decided then to share with Barbara, and this worked out well, with her using the bed and me the couch. On the day the Pope was to arrive, it was so foggy that he could not land. The disappointment was palpable.

The second occasion for the papal visit happened the following year. This time Barbara, a doctor, an ambulance driver, and I drove in the new Rae ambulance to Fort Simpson. This trip took a few hours. Barbara and I were housed in the same place. She, again, was assigned day duty, and again, I was on nights. Fort Simpson had been mobbed all week with people who were very excited. Being on nights, I had missed much of the excitement. On the morning the Pope was to arrive, however, those of us working on nights moved the patients, who were able to be moved, onto gurneys and transported them in ambulances to the field set up to greet him. We were placed as near the podium as possible. It was too bad that Barbara had not been on nights, as I was the one who was within a few feet of the pontiff.

On our drive back to Rae, following the Pope's visit, we stopped the ambulance at the home of a family the doctor in our group knew. There, we enjoyed tea and snacks, which broke up the journey.

Later that year Barbara and I drove to Vancouver for a holiday. We had to leave late, so we stayed in Hay River at a small convent with two Gray Nuns, for a night. Driving on to Edmonton early the next day, we found no one at home in the large convent. It turned out that all the sisters were out cheering the Oilers, who had just won the Stanley Cup for the first time. From there, we drove on to Vancouver, where we stayed at one of the convents belonging to Barbara's order. I left the next morning to catch the ferry to Victoria where I visited my brother and future sister-in-law. It had been several years since I had seen them. We spent nearly a week together before I returned to Vancouver and then Barbara and I took the long journey back to Rae-Edzo.

* * *

I continued to see Barbara often even after leaving Rae-Edzo. My boss, who Sister Louise had warned me about, had become more and more difficult to deal with on a day to day basis. She shouted often at all the staff and accused us on several occasions of many things she deemed unacceptable. No matter how ridiculous her accusations were she would never back down. This made it impossible to continue working in that office. I was lucky as I could make a move, but others who had family and homes in Rae had to endure the harassment. Barbara and I had become friends, and it meant leaving her on her own, which her order was not keen on.

Once I got established in Yellowknife, I bought a car and was therefore able to drive to Rae-Edzo to visit. The cottage hospital was closed soon after I left and Barbara, then head nurse, had the task of moving into Rae where a new clinic and nurses' apartments had been built. She lived and worked there for a few more months and then was transferred to Saskatchewan.

I went to visit Barbara the first Spring she was there. I flew from Yellowknife to Edmonton, transferred to another flight to Fort McMurray, and then took a charter to La Loche near to where the Big C reserve, her post, was situated. She showed me around, and then next day, we set off to visit other sisters. There were two groups of nuns to visit, and we visited them both, in Meadow Lake and North Battleford, before driving back. We had a week in and around La Loche and then I had a repeat journey back to Yellowknife.

Barbara and I met in Edmonton one more time. I flew in from Yellowknife, and she flew in from Saskatchewan. We attended a conference about Enneagrams, which was a way of looking at personality types and was very popular at that time. During that visit, the sisters were having a big celebration. They all left to go to church and asked me to watch Sister Elizabeth, who had Alzheimer's. At one point, she disappeared, and I spent a long time searching for her. Eventually, there she was in the chapel. She told me she was "Just saying hello to the Lord."

Barbara moved back to New Brunswick, to her motherhouse in Saint John, and then found work in the Miramichi area from where her family had come. She was the baby of fifteen children and had many family members still living in the area. While working in Fredericton, she was diagnosed with breast cancer. I flew to be with her some time after she had had a mastectomy. She picked me up at the airport, and I was amazed to see that her once blond curly hair was now coming in straight and dark. She continued to work, and I went with her to the several reserves she was looking after. We also visited, on her time off, several of her family. She showed me around the area, especially the university where she had done her degree.

She did well, but the cancer returned, five years later, and she had another mastectomy. I again returned to New Brunswick, this time to Saint John. By then, she had stopped working for the federal government and was looking after the elderly sisters in their nursing home. We had a holiday at the retreat house on the Saint John River that the order had provided for the nuns' use. Two other sisters were there at the time. Barbara and I took long walks through the woods, went to a fall supper at the church hall, and borrowed the car to visit St. Andrew and St. Stephen. One night, I had to get up to use the bathroom. It was dark, and as I turned a corner, I bumped into a big statue of St. Anthony. I let out a scream and woke up the household. The sisters thought it was hilarious and told everybody they met. That holiday was the last time I saw Barbara. We phoned regularly, and I always knew that when the phone rang late at night, it would be Barbara. The phone booth in the convent was in a cupboard which gave Barbara some privacy. When she could not sleep, she would phone. I spoke to her two days before she died. A letter from one of the other sisters informed me of her death. I still miss her at times, even after all these years. We had a unique, unusual, but close friendship.

The Boss, and the Voice

My first encounter with my boss was outside the clinic in Rae, where she stood in the snow, dressed in a parka, scarf, mitts, and hat, and yet, she still looked cold. Her black skin betrayed her inheritance and gave a clue to her discomfort in this cold, isolated place. Lithe, with long legs and dark rather piercing eyes, she dominated the area. Her reputation, which had been relayed by the bush telegraph and I had known long beforehand, when Sister Louise had asked for a transfer, and she explained her reasoning. We shook hands and started a wary, but necessary relationship. She was my boss, and I had to get used to the situation.

We worked well in the beginning, getting to know the fly-in communities, travelling together to find the needs of each and establishing a routine. Clinics needed to be opened, contacts made, and living places made more comfortable. In one place old school desk tops were provided, for our sleeping bags to be laid on as the floor was too cold. As the days progressed, we determined what was needed, how often each village needed to be visited, how we would get there, and who would be the main practitioner. She did manage to get much accomplished, and our living spaces were made more livable after a time.

In one community I encountered the Voice. Phone call after phone call, night after night, he pestered. "I love you" was spoken in a drunken, slurred voice and repeated over and over. I knew who it was, but that did not help. Working in isolation in a village far from anything I had known, where another language was spoken, I felt very alone. I had been working in Lac La Marte, one of my fly-in communities north of Rae-Edzo, for several months, flying in on a Tuesday and staying until Thursday evening.

I normally felt quite safe, despite the trailer — where I lived and worked — being situated at the end of the village. It was barely adequate for a clinic, never mind a place to live, but that was what was provided. I had a room on one side, and the clinic was on the other. There was no running water in the winter. The tank on top of the trailer was filled with water from the lake by a truck once the ice melted. Both me and the patients had to use what was known as a "honey bucket" for a toilet. This consisted of a big bucket with a plastic lining. It had to be emptied on a regular basis. The trailer was heated and had a bed, stove, and small sofa. We had to bring any food we needed with us to the community, although were able to leave dry goods between trips.

The phone calls from the voice were persistent and threatening making me feel that the trailer was a vulnerable place to spend nights. I never quite knew if the "voice" would arrive in the middle of the night or if the phone calls were just for his amusement. Clients came to the door of my room to get attention any time they wanted after clinic hours were over. I was on call twenty-four hours a day. People often came to the trailer during the night with one excuse or another. Sometimes there was a real health problem, but at other times, it was just a place to come and spend time.

The sun never really went down in the summer, so people were out at all hours. Kids played outside night and day, shouting, screaming, and laughing. Sleep was a luxury as the door was likely to be pounded on at the least expected times.

I did not know the chief well — or anybody else of authority, at that time — and the RCMP only came into the community sporadically. I continued to travel to Lac La Marte on a twice monthly basis, working during the day at a clinic with people who needed treatment or were just there to hang out, visiting their friends. I had an interpreter, Mary Rose, who worked with me throughout the day and helped translate Dogrib, which the majority of people spoke, however she went home at the end of a normal clinic day. At night, I was alone in the other half of the trailer.

Although I was in the community regularly, I was there to work and as a result I did not get to know the people socially. As a result, and after much deliberation over the phone calls, I came to the conclusion that my only choice was to tell my boss. My stamina was faltering with sleep loss, work, and the constant pestering. At night, I was on my own on call, and I had to answer the phone or talk through the door in case it was an emergency. My harasser knew this.

On the next trip back to base, I plucked up some courage and told my boss my problem. She did pay attention, and despite our difficulties working together, she agreed to accompany me on the next trip. She planned to fly in and out in the same day. On my next routine visit, we flew onto the lake and marched to the trailer carrying our extra equipment, which was mainly the survival gear that we were obliged to carry on each trip and medications. We dealt with the people who were lined up for treatments, and then we went to see the "voice" at his home. The boss pulled herself to her imposing height — she was probably nearly six feet — gave him her most piercing look, and told him, using some choice language, never to harass me again or she would deal with him.

My boss' reputation had travelled fast, and the unknown was probably worse than the reality. It worked; her weird, volatile personality gave him and many others a scare. Life, for me, calmed down after that, and I was at last able to get some genuine sleep. I didn't have any more of those phone calls.

I continued to work in Lac La Marte for many months without more problems. Sometime later, while working in Yellowknife, I was asked to return there for two weeks to fill in for the nurse who was going on holiday. In Yellowknife, we worked in our community nurse capacity but we also took turns to be on call, sometimes needing to travel all over the western Arctic to medevac patients who needed more extensive treatment than the local nurse was able to provide. I had Friday as my travel day and was therefore flying almost every week. We were also asked on occasions to fill in for nurses who were going on holiday. Married nurses with children were rarely asked to go which meant that I, as a single woman, often got the job.

When asked to return to Lac La Marte for my only trip back, I had argued with the nursing officer about being sent alone. She reluctantly agreed that another nurse would be allowed to accompany me for the two weeks we were assigned. I wondered if my harasser still lived there. At the place where the plane landed, we received the keys from the nurse who was now permanently in the community. On our quick turnaround, she gave us a brief summary about what was happening and assured us that her notes would keep us up-to-date. There were no immediate worries, just the usual routine health problems. She flew off, and we made our way to the nursing station with our belongings, some food, and a small radio. By then, there was a proper nursing station. Provided now was a nurse's apartment upstairs and a clinic downstairs. It was a safer place, with an intercom installed. The clinic went on as usual, with many people coming in with all the usual ailments. There was an outbreak of scabies among many of the children. As there was hot water in the nursing station by this time, many children were treated there. Either parents came in and we soaked the children together, or we did it ourselves with their permission. Everybody felt so good after a nice warm bath and some topical cream.

One night, a woman came in with her baby, who was coughing and coughing. We realized that he had croup and needed to be in a croupette to give him some moisture and help him open his nasal passages. We placed him in the cot with the apparatus at the bottom. It had to be filled up with water and then plugged in so it could heat up and provide steam. I began to fill it up, but soon realized that the base of the water container had rusted, and we had water all over the floor. Relying on some makeshift ingenuity, we covered the cot with a sheet and placed a kettle near the bottom of the cot. This provided enough steam to help with the breathing. Once he was settled and started on treatment, and we were happy with his progress, we decided to go to bed. The mother of the baby slept on the bed next to the child and kept an eye on him. She knew to wake one of us up anytime she was worried. He slept, she slept, and the other nurse and I slept for short times, keeping our alarm on at intervals to get either of us up to check his progress. He remained in clinic for quite a few hours the next day before we sent him home. A requisition for a new croupette was put in as soon as we got back to headquarters.

One the first Sunday of our stay a group of men came banging on the door late one morning. A man had collapsed at church and some thought that he was having a heart attack. They grabbed a stretcher, rushed back to the church, and brought him in to clinic. Together we got him onto a bed. He looked pale and his breathing was laboured. We examined him and came to the conclusion that there was not too much to worry about. We suspected that it was probably too hot in the church, and he had fainted. At that time, men wore their caribou skin jackets in church and women wore different jackets, but always with a blue scarf on their heads. They often lit candles during the ceremony. With the candles, and the extra clothing, church regularly became unbearably hot.

After some time, by laying still and resting, the patient's breathing and other vitals reverted to normal. I made a big pot of tea, provided some cups, and proceeded to supply the many people who had turned up to see what was going on. Often, when patients were admitted, many family members came to the room. This was no exception. It seemed that the best cure for a "heart attack" on that day was tea.

One of the days when I had been seeing clients in clinic all morning, I came out to get the next in line and realized that the "voice" was sitting there, looking at me. He needed help, as he had cut his hand with an axe. Blood was seeping through the dish cloth that he had wrapped his injured hand in. He came into the clinic room, and I proceeded to unwrap the hand, finding a big gash that needed to be stitched. After cleaning and disinfecting the wound, I started to close the gap. I was tempted to make each stitch hurt, but resisted and used the appropriate local anesthetic. He was treated like any other patient. After cleaning, stitching, and bandaging the wound, he was on his way. Nothing was said by either of us about our past encounter.

The week went on with no other memorable incidents. I returned to Yellowknife having seen and treated the "voice." We had left things without a fuss. I did hear that he still lived in the same place. Whether he harassed any other nurse I will never know.

The boss revealed bit by bit, mainly when driving and travelling, to having been a dancer in her younger years, she also mentioned having talent in drawing. These abilities could have been celebrated, used to promote her own happiness, or extended to create a bridge between her and others. However, the darker side of her character seeped through day by day.

Her personality slowly came to the fore over the months, revealing a vicious streak, which she exhibited more and more often. Daily work became tentative, with each day a new experience, depending on her mood. Shouting at staff became routine; deliberate refusal for the staff to use equipment was often exerted. Leaving to travel to another community, despite the isolation and work involved, became the only way to feel relief and get any rest from the constant humiliation and accusations. As she became more and more difficult to be around, I found myself dreaming and using books and art to travel to places of magic and intrigue.

She lived two doors down and kept an eye on all of us, including those who worked in the hospital. She liked to interfere with the lives of as many people as possible, creating havoc on occasions. She was supposed to pick me up in the mornings and drive to the next village, where we had our clinic and office. This happened most days, but sporadically she would ignore me, and I ended up hitchhiking to work. This occurred many times, and I became quite well known on the road, with my thumb out. I never got an excuse as to why I was not picked up as usual, just a blasting about being late.

We did travel to Yellowknife for a nurse's conference together on one occasion. Things were going well until, for some reason, the chamber maid in the boss' room hung up a piece of clothing that had been dropped. Angry that someone had touched her clothes, she not only complained to the manager, but left the conference and drove back to Rae-Edzo. This left me stranded with no way back. Eventually, I phoned Barbara and she made the long drive to fetch me.

On another occasion, the boss went to Ottawa for a conference, which she extended for a holiday. She had taken with her drafts of health posters I had developed. I had worked on them for weeks in my spare time. I had gathered information, drawn out my ideas, and shown them to people around the community. She had approved of them and agreed to take them with her to Ottawa. It was a relieved when she left. Three weeks of driving myself to work, having the car anytime I needed it, and not having to explain where I was going was a welcome experience. I agreed to look after her place while she was away, which meant I had a few plants to water. She had an obsession with African violets and had many, all different colours throughout her house.

On her return, I picked her up to drive her home. She seemed pleased to tell me some of the details of her trip and was full of the people she had seen, who had taken her for dinner, what some of the discussions were about at the conference. I asked if the draft of the health posters I had developed had been viewed by her contacts. She told me that they had been approved and would be printed.

"All is well at the house" I said, as we drove into the driveway outside the small house where she lived. "The plants survived." We entered the living room with the luggage and set it down on the mustard-coloured carpet that I had vacuumed that morning.

The next morning, she picked me up for work. She informed me that she had inspected each African violet plant and was furious as I had apparently allowed one to lose some of its leaves. She had counted all the leaves on each plant and now accused me of neglect. I could not believe that I was being blamed for something that happens often with any plant.

A few weeks later, my patience was tested. The day had finally arrived when the posters were being delivered. Several of us crowded around as the box was opened. I could not believe my eyes when I saw them. On the bottom was her name, instead of mine.

Life became unbearable, and I soon learned when I went to a conference that I had gained a reputation as the only person to work more than a few months with the boss. A very perverted notoriety! I lasted a few more months, but eventually work life became so unbearable that I asked for a transfer and was lucky enough to find a job fairly quickly in Yellowknife. She moved sometime after I left and on that occasion was sent to a very remote Inuit community to work alone. I learned many years later that she had died of a brain tumor.

The Convent

I felt very fortunate to get work in Yellowknife so quickly until I was told there was no accommodation available. The nurse I was replacing was married to a teacher, and they had been living in the teacher's housing.

Barbara and I had been to the convent in Yellowknife on at least a couple of occasions for dinner, and we had also stayed overnight. The nuns there knew me. Barbara phoned them and asked if I could stay with them until a new apartment was located. The sisters discussed it, and it was agreed that I could live with them for a short time.

I packed up and, with Barbara's help, moved into the city and my new interesting home. I was given a room on the second floor, where all the bedrooms were located. Mine was above the chapel, so I had to get used to early morning singing. The room reminded me of my student nurse days in Glasgow, except it had no sink. A narrow single bed, a small clothes closet, and a bedside table were the only contents. The one difference in this room was a huge cross on the wall at the head of the bed. At first I found it jarring, but soon got used to it.

At that time, there were seven nuns living there. All but one were teachers in the local Catholic schools. The seventh was the cook and housekeeper. Only one wore a habit; Sister

Cornelius refused to change into regular clothing, despite it being no longer necessary. Although I paid rent, it was a luxury to have meals provided. We all helped with chores, including dishes, as there was no dishwasher. After supper, and when the sisters met in the chapel for prayers, I usually put the dishes away. We then all got together in the living room. On weekends, the whole place was cleaned, and if I was not out on call, I would be part of the cleaning crew. I was even allowed to clean in the chapel and did sneak a "holy" wafer when cleaning out the cupboard, just to see how it tasted.

At that time, we public health nurses were employed by the federal government, and in addition to our public health duties, we were expected to carry out all the medevacs for the western Arctic. I was given Friday as my on-call day, and we also took turns covering the weekends. This meant I was on call every Friday and every fifth weekend. On our on-call days, we went to work as usual carrying a pager. I always told the patient I was visiting that I was on call. Once the pager went off, no matter where I was, or what I was doing, I dropped everything, found a phone to let the office know where I was, and drove back to base. There I picked up the equipment needed and then was driven to the airport to board the plane assigned to me to fly to the community that needed a patient to be transported back to Yellowknife.

I often had to creep out of the convent at all hours to fly to anywhere within the western NWT. Since I was on call at the end of the week, if I disturbed anybody, they were able to return to sleep. I was given a key to the convent in case my journey was short, however we very often had to fly for several hours to get the patient and return to Stanton Yellowknife Hospital. Having worked all day and then often half the night, I would return home exhausted. The convent was a good place to sleep during the day, as it was very quiet.

Being teachers, the sisters often had to prepare school work. I got involved and cut out many alphabet letters over time. I also helped make puppets and many other items that were needed. I have always liked to make things and, occasionally, was able to suggest a way to construct an item.

The priest lived in a residence attached to the church; however, he often came over to the convent for supper. He rarely joined the sisters, preferring to eat alone in his own dining room. He was feted, and the nuns were very deferential to him and his needs. He left a couple of months after I moved into the convent. Another priest replaced him soon after, and he was very different from the previous one. The new priest was more friendly and preferred to cook for himself, only coming to eat at the convent for special occasions. He probably ate with parishioners, so he did not have to cook too often. He came skiing with us and joined in many parties and other events. Eventually, it became apparent that he had fallen in love with one of the girls from Dettah, a nearby village. They both came to the convent frequently, and the attachment could not be hidden. The liaison caused a scandal in the city, but was quelled when Father asked for dispensation from the Vatican. This was eventually granted, and a wedding was planned. At first, the sisters were reluctant to attend, but as the couple were friends, they relented. They all attended, as did I. The service was performed out in the country at a restaurant near summer cabins. The people from Dettah attended, but refused to wear their best clothes as a way of letting others know how they felt about the situation. As far as I know, the couple still live in Dettah and have three children.

***

I enjoyed many things with the sisters either at the convent while living there, or at my place once I finally got a place of my own. They knew a great many people from the church or who worked in the schools they taught and I was often included in many of the gatherings.

There was a large Filipino community in Yellowknife at that time, and they knew the sisters from church. We enjoyed many parties with them. When we occasionally had a beer and movie night, I was the one who was sent to get the beer at the liquor store.

One of the things I learned to appreciate during my time at the convent was that the sisters celebrated many occasions. As a single woman with no family, they encouraged me to celebrate many different personal events. Apart from, birthdays, their saints' days were all noted and a cause for a special meal and, often, cake. Theme parties were frequently a hit. We had beach parties, Roman parties, skiing parties, and many more, all inside. Decorations were often made, and occasionally, we dressed up in the appropriate costumes. All the usual holidays were also enjoyed.

I stayed in the convent for about four and a half months before getting my own apartment. This was just in time, as the sisters all went back to their motherhouse in London, Ontario, for the summer, and I would have had to have found new temporary accommodation.

I often returned to visit, and the sisters also came to my place to continue our friendship. I would put on a large pot of chili when they visited, which we enjoyed together.

My friendship with the sisters was strong and we helped each other out .When relatives of the sisters' came to visit, they had to find other accommodation as there were only single beds at the convent and men were not allowed. As I had a one-bedroom apartment, I returned to the convent on those occasions, allowing the visitors to enjoy a place of their own.

One of the families in the church had a cabin at a nearby lake, which the nuns were able to use. I was asked to join them a few times. We had a great time out in the bush, taking pleasure in the quiet and nature. One time, one of the sisters and I went out early to camp, and the others came the next day. She and I were the only ones of the group who enjoyed sardines, which were deemed distasteful by the other sisters, so we made sure we took tins with us, to enjoy without hearing remarks from the others.

At some point during my first year in Yellowknife, I joined the Choral Society. We put on regular choral concerts, and on two occasions, we did some acting. *Trial by Jury*, a Gilbert and Sullivan operetta was one. We jurists were kitted out with elaborate costumes, which included large hats. The other event was one written by one of the local music teachers, with the cooperation of our conductor. The leading man was very tall, and I, being very short, was given the part to act as his alter ego. The sisters all came to the performance to cheer me on.

My parents came to visit me when they came to Canada for a holiday. They had been in Canada on a few occasions, but never so far north. I took time off to spend with them. We spent one week in Yellowknife, and then flew to Victoria to spend a family holiday with my brother and his wife. In Yellowknife, we had dinner at the convent, which was quite an eye-opener for my folks. They, like me previously, had never met a nun and were so surprised to find out that they were ordinary, interesting women. At the time I was growing up in Scotland the Protestant/Catholic divide was very strong with little understanding or tolerance of the other religion.

Two annual events were enjoyed by the sisters and all of Yellowknife each year. In the Spring, we attended the Ice Festival, where amazing ice sculptures were created. There were also all kinds of food booths, fun stalls, and dogsled rides. On the twenty-first of June, the whole town came to a halt to celebrate midsummer. There was a parade, and everybody stayed up much of the night on the street, as the daylight continued all night. They we would go back to the convent to have food and continue the celebration.

A new bishop was elected for the North. He decided to make his headquarters in Yellowknife and requested the use of the convent. As a result, the sisters had to find a new place to live. Why one man needed an eight-bedroom house was a mystery. Eventually, after a lot of work, a new home was found to rent in, of all places, "School Draw," an appropriate road for teachers. It was slightly further from the church and the schools, but not too far. It was a great location, overlooking the lake. By then, one of the teaching sisters had left, as had the cook. The sisters who stayed had to adapt to new circumstances and work to a schedule, as they now all took turns cooking.

For my first five years in NWT I had been employed by the Federal Government. Once the Northwest Territories government took over the health department we no longer had to do medevacs, leaving my Friday nights and weekends free. I often went down to the new convent after work on a Friday, sometime taking my laundry and PJs with me.

In the winter, once the lake had frozen over, many of the sisters and I were able to ski along the lake and around some of the small islands normally surrounded by water. We would then return to the convent for hot chocolate. Around Christmas time, we would get together, with a few other people, and go out Christmas carolling up one side of School Draw and down the other. We were offered food and drinks on the way. Full and happy, we ended up at one house, once the carolling was over, where we continued to party. We then made our way back to the convent, late in the night or early morning, to sleep.

Sister Cornelius, the nun who still wore a habit, moved over during the time the big convent was their home, to live in a room attached to the small church in Dettah. While there, she and I worked together on several projects. One of these was to get money together to send some children to the Expo taking place in Vancouver the following year. One of the organized events was a bingo in one of the halls in Yellowknife.

On the night of the event, I worked in the kitchen making sandwiches and other food to sell. I was glad to be out of the main hall, as smoking was still allowed back then and the air was blue. At the end of the evening, I walked home, accompanied by the most amazing Aurora Borealis I was to ever witness. The whole sky was ablaze with dancing light of many colours. It took me a long time to walk home as I was in awe.

With the money we made, at the various money-making schemes, we were able to send six children and a chaperone to the Expo. None of the kids had ever been out of NWT, and it was, therefore, a huge experience in their lives. All of the sisters and I also visited Expo that year, living in the convent owned by Barbara's order in Vancouver. She had moved by then and was not part of the group. At the convent, we were packed into every space. I slept on the floor in the basement on a couple of cushions. We had a few days at Expo and enjoyed other things in Vancouver. One night, we went to Chinatown for a large Chinese meal. It was a memorable time for us all;

in a place few of us knew. The sisters flew back to Ontario for the summer, and I went on to Victoria to visit my brother.

***

I decided to move to Victoria as I had always liked it when visiting my brother. I needed to get my BScN to be allowed to work as a public health Nurse in BC. When I finally got accepted after sitting an entrance course, I had to clean my apartment in Yellowknife from top to bottom. The sisters came with cleaning materials and together we cleaned carpets, walls, and the kitchen area. I provided food and the normally onerous chore passed with ease. Before I left Yellowknife, I was given a ring, making me an honorary member of the Sisters of St Josephs of London. I had to get it sized, and during that procedure, I had the small cross taken off. I have worn that ring every day since receiving it.

Before moving to Victoria Sister Diane was given permission to accompany me to Europe and then Scotland for a holiday. We looked into many possibilities before deciding on a bus tour starting in London, travelling across the English Channel, and ending in Amsterdam. From there, it was on through to Germany, then Austria — where we spent a few nights — before finally arriving in Italy. There, we had a couple of days each in Venice, Florence, and Rome. From Italy, we were off again to Paris and then once again across the Channel to London. We had one night in London before travelling to Scotland by bus.

That particular bus journey proved to be very eventful. We choose to take a seat upstairs; as it gave us a great view. We travelled some distance before everyone began to feel very hot. The conductress eventually shouted that there was a problem with the air conditioning. People opened windows, but it did not help. Eventually, we stopped at a large garage where ice cream was bought for everybody on the bus. The heat did not improve, and at one time, a passenger lay on the floor trying to cool down. As we drove through the border, the bus exited the highway and drove onto narrow lanes. Why we will never know. Eventually, this was rectified, and we managed to get to Glasgow, where my parents had been waiting for a considerable time to pick us up.

Living in the convent and knowing the sisters was a great experience. The sisters are scattered all over the place now, but most are back in Ontario. I continue to be in touch with one of the nuns by letter and email, and she keeps me up-to-date with all their news. The nuns were among many interesting people I met when living and working in Yellowknife.

Mary Louise, Harriet and Jackie

I first met Mary Louise when I moved into Yellowknife from Rae-Edzo. I was assigned Rainbow Valley an area with houses just outside the main area of Yellowknife and Dettah, a village on Great Slave Lake that was totally Indigenous and about thirty minutes by road, and ten minutes by ice road, from Yellowknife. There were, at that time, about ninety people living in Dettah. The village had a small, one teacher, elementary school, a tiny church, a village hall, a trailer where I had my clinic, and many houses.

Mary Louise became my community liaison and my interpreter as the majority of the people who lived in Dettah and Rainbow Valley spoke Dogrib. I learned to be patient when asking a question about a client as it often seemed that more than my question was being discussed. Eventually I got a reply and we dealt with the need.

I was expected to drive a large van with three rows of seats. This caused me some problems, but with cushions behind my back, I was able to just reach the pedals. I was not supposed to give people lifts, however, this was done fairly often once I got to know people. My new boss knew that this occurred, but as long as she did not see it happening, she turned a blind eye. As a result, I had to drop people off before we reached the public health office.

I was only in my new job for a week before the staff in the health unit was told that they would be going out to cabins at a nearby lake to learn some alternative medicine techniques. On one week, the Indigenous support staff were to go and the following week, the nurses. Since I would be working closely with Indigenous people, I asked to go with them on the trip, instead of with the other nursing staff. We were taken out to the cabins where we met up with staff from all over the Territories. There was one Inuit man, and the rest were women.

It was the middle of April and very cold, but we were all used to it. After meeting and eating, we were shown to our cabins. I was to share a cabin with two ladies: Mary Louise and Martha. During the day, we learned Qigong and other methods of alternative medicine. None of us had done anything like it before, but we all stretched and pushed ourselves, learning the various moves and reasons behind them. At night after supper, we got together and told stories, sometimes in the Dogrib language, sometimes in one of the other northern languages. With sporadic English and despite not knowing each other's languages, we laughed a lot, sometimes to the point of tears. We had to take turns to keep the stove in the cabin going, waking each other every two hours to throw more logs on the fire. This was a great way to learn to trust others, as responsibility rested on everyone to keep the room warm.

We went for walks on our time off, and I learned from Mary Louise about the herbs, native plants, and medicines. She taught me how different plants were used as swabs to stop bleeding and for many assorted ailments. I also learned about Dettah, where she lived with her family and where she had been brought up and lived all her life. She was full of knowledge and was able to convey it with ease.

Into the Unknown

The Catholic Church in Dettah was a focal place for the community. The priest from Yellowknife came out to have Mass every Sunday afternoon. Weddings and other events took place here despite it being small.

The week, following learning about alternative medicine methods, I continued my time in Dettah feeling that I had a friend to work with and happy that I had made the decision to join the support staff on the course. It was not until a few weeks into my new job that I realized Mary Louise could not read or write English. At that time, Dogrib was not a written language, so that was also not a possibility for her. I was surprised as it had never crossed my mind that this knowledgeable person could not do something I took for granted. Gradually, I learned why this had happened. She was of an age when children were taken from their homes and put in residential schools. Each time the boat came to take the children from the village, her parents had hidden her in the woods. This happened many times, and each year, her family managed to hide her. This meant that Mary Louise never had a formal education and never learned to read or write.

It is difficult to imagine what her life would have been like if, in fact, she had gone to school and learned to read and write. She, after all, had a full life, and with her husband, had brought up four children who had all gone on to further their education beyond high school. They had a lovely house that she had helped to build, and she held down a regular job. It must have taken a great deal of ingenuity to overcome situations that required written instructions. We wrote her reports together, with her telling me what she wanted recorded and me doing the recording.

Mary Louise's ability to learn by observing, listening and practising skills, made her into a teacher who willingly shared her extensive knowledge with others. She met Margaret Atwood's goal of building knowledge upon knowledge without the privilege of learning to read and write. If she had learned to read and write in a residential school, what damage would she have suffered personally? She would have no doubt lost her language and maybe her self-esteem, or worse.

As part of my work, I had to teach "health" topics at the school. The one teacher used to spend the time that I was engaged with the students in his office, leaving me to cope on my own. After the first class, where I don't think the children paid much attention, I made sure Mary Louise came with me. One word from her in their own language, and they sat up and really listened. After that, we planned classes together and found ways to teach the various topics in a more appropriate way, one that the children could understand and be interested in.

One of the things that Mary Louise wanted to do was to get a bank book. We talked about this on occasion, and finally, on one of the days we were in town together, we went into the bank. With the paperwork completed, a bank book was procured. Mary Louise was proud to show it to people. Although she did not put a great deal of money into it, it somehow made her feel good.

We worked together for five years. During that time, I learned a lot about native plants and Indigenous ways and was lucky enough to participate in many Indigenous activities. Those included attending and dancing at many drum dances. I was honoured to be given an Indigenous name. Unfortunately, it is in the Dogrib language and therefore cannot be recorded. It means Little Sister.

The week I left to go to university in Victoria for two years, at the end of August 1990, I had dinner with Mary Louise and her family, and they gave me a vest and a pair of moccasins that Mary Louise had beaded. I was excited to be at last going to university but knew that I would be missing all the friends I had made in Yellowknife and the clients I had got to know in the two a districts I was assigned.

Mary Louise and I met again one more time the following year, when I came to work in Rae for the summer. I worked there for nine weeks straight, followed by two weeks in Fort Liard. I then returned to Yellowknife for a week to house- and cat-sit for friends. They had gone on holiday and left me the car. I visited many friends during that time, including those in Dettah. Mary Louise had had her house renovated with money supplied by the winnings from the lottery her daughter had received some months previously. A more modern kitchen and other updated conveniences were obvious. She and her husband, Johnny, were happy to show me all the new gadgets and house improvements. After a good visit, I was asked to return the next day for a picnic with them and one of their grandchildren. I returned to Dettah at the agreed time, and we piled into their boat with our food to sail over to one of the islands. On the way, some ducks flew over. Johnny immediately grabbed his gun and with one shot, got a duck. It fell into the lake and we picked it up before going on our way.

Arriving on the island, we collected wood and kindling for the fire. We cooked caribou and various vegetables flavoured by herbs Mary Louise had found. We then had dessert, which I had brought. It was a great trip that I enjoyed thoroughly. As usual, I had learned from them. That day I learned about herbs and outdoor cooking and was entertained with tales of camping.

This was the last trip I took to the North, and after thirty years, I know very few people there. I did see on the television an item about Dettah when Prince Charles and Camilla visited, in the Spring of 2022. Mary Louise's grandson had become a prominent member of the community, and the large, new community centre was named after the family.

* * *

After I moved to Yellowknife and had started to visit Dettah on a weekly basis I met Harriet and her husband Joe. The clinic trailer where I had my office was across from Harriet and Joe's home. On my first visit, Mary Louise, my interpreter, took me around the community, introducing me to as many people as possible. Harriet and Joe were our first call. Their house was typical of the kind of home that was found in northern Indigenous communities. Immediately upon opening the front door, a wood stove was in view. To one side stood a couch, a couple of chairs, and often a television and a table. A bed, surrounded by a curtain, was placed behind the stove. Another bed, usually taking up the whole room, was walled off but the wall did not necessarily reach the ceiling. There was kitchen space behind the couch, and the bathroom was also walled off. Very little space was available.

I met Harriet for the first time during one of her more stable periods. She had been diagnosed with a psychiatric problem several years previously. I got to know her well as she needed to have an injection weekly to keep her on an even keel. She and Joe had been married for a long time and had three children and several grandchildren. Joe worked and Harriet stayed home to manage the house and be involved helping with grandchildren. Some days, she was well and allowed Mary Louise and me in without a problem; others, she needed to be persuaded. It took a fair amount of time for us to develop a relationship, but with patience and weekly visits, we fell into an understanding. Eventually, I was able to call on her by myself.

On one of these one-on-one occasions, Harriet met me at the door. The stove was bright red and overheating, and the house extremely hot. I remarked on this and was answered with a big bowl of frozen berries to cool me down. Harriet insisted that I eat them all before I was allowed to give her the injection. Throughout my stay, she insisted on putting more and more wood in the stove. I worried that she would burn the house down. Once I was able to leave the house, I went to one of her neighbour's homes to tell them what was happening. They agreed to keep an eye on the situation.

Another incident occurred during the winter. I was woken in the middle of the night by a phone call from a nurse at the hospital. Harriet had been admitted that afternoon. Despite her being given meds to calm her down, she was still pacing the corridors, annoying other patients. Somehow, my name came up, and the staff wondered if I could come to the ward to try and get her to rest.

A taxi was sent for me. I got up, dressed for the cold, and waited in the foyer of my building. Eventually, my transportation arrived and took me to the hospital. I was ushered to the appropriate floor and found Harriet wandering around. She was in a hospital gown, but had bare feet. I took her hand and led her back to her room. Persuading her to sit on the bed, I talked to her quietly, held her hand with one of my hands while brushing her arms with the other. Harriet responded, and without more agitation, she lay down. I stayed with her until she fell asleep. The staff and I were amazed.

The Chief's house in Dettah. The Chiefs in Dettah were elected every few years. A flagpole was erected outside the home of each new chief. The flag had the colours of NWT with a native design in the middle.

Into the Unknown

Harriet and Joe had a daughter, Mary Rose, whom I knew well. She had epilepsy and an alcohol addiction. She often came to the Yellowknife clinic to see me, frequently asking for cough syrup, which often contained alcohol. This was a common request of the street population as it was mixed with cheap wine to make an enhanced cocktail. On one of these occasions, Mary Rose began to have a seizure. I jumped up to hold her up on her chair, which was opposite to me. She was a big girl, however, and fell forward, pinning me to the floor. Fortunately, one of the other nurses heard my shout for help and came to my rescue. No harm was done to me or to Mary Rose, but it was nonetheless a frightening, yet funny experience. Mary Rose was embarrassed.

One day, word came in that Mary Rose had been found some distance from town, on the side of the road, dead. She had been murdered, and mutilated, the night before. We were all shocked. Her sister came to the clinic to ask if anything could be done about reaching her parents, who were out on their trap line. After much discussion and many phone calls, it was agreed that the RCMP helicopter would take the sister and me to the trap line to bring Harriet and Joe back. It was my first time on a helicopter, but I did not appreciate the experience as I was too worried about the reception we would get. We eventually found a clearing near their camp and set down. When we walked into the campsite the pair was waiting for us. They had heard the drone of the chopper and, of course, wondered what we were doing out so far and why.

Harriet surprisingly took the news better than her husband. We bundled up their equipment and furs into the helicopter and flew back to Yellowknife. The RCMP took over from there, and I went back to the clinic. It took a few months to get the details of what had happened that night. The culprit, who was a taxi driver, was not from the area. He was apprehended in Toronto, where he had flown after the incident. Harriet remained stoic for some time, but broke down at the funeral, which took place in the small church in the village.

Harriet and I had a different relationship after that. She allowed me to treat her weekly and to see her at her vulnerable times. She liked to hold my hand and when in good spirits, loved to tease. I often think of her, but as she was quite a bit older than me, and it was over thirty years ago, I imagine she is no longer living.

***

Like many street people in Yellowknife, Jackie used to congregate on the steps of the post office on the main street, fairly near the public health office. If we needed to find someone, it was the first place we looked. When they were not there, someone either knew where they were or were willing to tell them we were looking for them. Jackie often sat there, and we acknowledged each other on many occasions.

Over the months, we got to know each other, and she often came into the clinic. Sometimes she came just to keep warm, sometimes to have a cup of coffee from the pot we always had brewing, but mostly she just came to talk. Gradually, I got to know some of her story. She had an alcohol problem, and although her mother lived in Rainbow Valley, where many Indigenous people lived, Jackie slept rough much of the time.

Jackie was not from the area, being a Chipewyan from northern Alberta. She had moved to Yellowknife with her mother and siblings years earlier. She was once married, but had no children. The marriage ended when she murdered her husband in an alcohol-fueled fight. Self-defence was taken into consideration, and she had spent two years less a day in prison. Despite her background, her physical power, and gruffness, I saw in Jackie someone who had had a terrible early life, with few highlights or any encouragement. Despite that, she had a kind heart.

Just before I had moved to the city, Jackie's sister had died in a tent fire, leaving a baby daughter, Elizabeth. Jackie decided that she wanted to have that baby who was now over a year and living in a foster home. She talked over the possibility with many people, including me. The first thing that was suggested was for her to get sober. We had a detox centre in Yellowknife at that time, but it had a long waiting list. Gradually, her name came to the top of the list, and she was admitted. The first attempt at sobering up did not last, but with some pleading on my behalf and the reassurance that I would give her support, she was readmitted. She did well on the second attempt.

While Jackie was at the detox centre, she met John, who had been sober for some time and was now working there. John was from Rae, and although I knew his family, he had not lived in the area for some time, and I had not met him previously. John and Jackie hit it off and agreed to live together once her detox was completed.

The couple managed to find a very small piece of land in Rainbow Valley and, together, built a tiny house. They had one room with an inset for a bed, a place to cook, and a toilet and sink. Despite the size, they managed to fill it with enough furniture to be comfortable. They were both very proud of their new home. Some months passed and Jackie remained sober. With the help of social services, my advocating for the couple, and completing extensive paperwork, Elizabeth was handed over to them on a trial basis. I agreed to visit them twice a week and did this for a lengthy period of time. Throughout the months, it was obvious that Elizabeth was being well cared for and loved.

Jackie, and sometimes John came to the clinic for all of Elizabeth's immunizations and health checks. From the beginning, it was clear that Elizabeth had problems, and eventually, she was diagnosed with Fetal Alcohol Syndrome. She had no obvious physical problems at first, but over time may have developed sight and hearing problems. Once at school she had difficulties with attention and impulse control. This made no difference to how Jackie and John felt about their little girl.

One March, I was coming back from getting my driver's licence renewed when I spotted Jackie. I asked her where she was going, and eventually, she told me she was going to the liquor store. I asked her to sit with me for a while. We sat on a low wall, and she told me she was very upset as her friend Doreen had been murdered by her husband. Doreen lived in Dettah, and she and her family were well known to me. Jackie and I were therefore able to talk about Doreen and how much she meant to Jackie. We talked and talked and then realized that we were both frozen. I suggested that we go to a nearby café for a coffee, and Jackie agreed. We had the coffee and thawed out. I had to go back to work and asked Jackie if she had a plan. She decided to catch the bus and go home. The possible return to drinking had been averted, and we had had a chance to discuss an event that we both needed to talk about.

During my summer break from university, I went back North to work and I was able to visit Jackie, John, and Elizabeth. They continued to live in their tiny home, and with John working, they were able to have the extra things they needed. At the end of my visit, we agreed to meet up in town and have lunch before I went back to Victoria. I asked Jackie where she wanted to go. She thought for a while and then asked me if we could go to a certain restaurant on the main street. She had always wanted to go there, she told me. On the appointed day, I was at the restaurant early and got a table. It was not a particularly special place, but when Jackie and Elizabeth arrived, they were in their very best clothes. Jackie was really pleased to be eating in a place she had previously thought she would not be accepted in. As a street person, she may not have been allowed in, but now things had changed, and she had pulled her life together. She had become a mother and a wife, and she had a home of her own.

I learned a few years later from one of the nuns that John, Jackie and Elizabeth had been in a horrible accident. They had been driving home from Rae-Edzo when John hit the thick gravel at the side of the road. The car had rolled and John had died. Jackie and Elizabeth survived, and as far as I know, despite difficulties, they continued to live in Rainbow Valley. Elizabeth would be in her thirties now, but not knowing anybody in Yellowknife, I have no idea how she and Jackie are doing.

Flying

Every person who worked for the federal government and flew as part of their job was required to take a survival course. Eventually, one April, it was my turn. It turned out that I was the only health staff present, as the other seven had a variety of occupations.

We went to a classroom for a day to learn the theory of survival before being driven out to the wilderness for an overnight stay. On the morning of the practical, we all piled into a truck and drove and drove. Eventually, we stopped in an area with a few trees. We had with us a survival kit, a parachute, two sleeping bags, a first aid box, matches, a tin mug, a camping pot, some tea and a few dried foods — which could be hydrated and made into a soup if a fire was started — were unloaded with us. We were also given a rifle and some wire from which rabbit snares were expected to be fashioned.

Our first strategy was to set up some kind of shelter using the parachute. We draped it over some branches and secured it with rope that was found in the kit. As there were only two sleeping bags, we had to take turns to sleep; therefore the shelter could be small.

Sticks were found and eventually we got a fire going. A pot of water from a great deal of melted snow was boiled and tea was made. Later, we made soup, and as we only had one mug, had to take turns drinking and eating.

We also built a second shelter by forming a huge mound out of snow. Once it was big enough to shelter one or two people, sticks of the same length were gathered. These were pushed all around and into the top of the pile. We then scooped and scooped from the base, creating a snow shelter. When we saw the ends of the sticks we knew when to stop as the dome thickness was measured. We managed to make it big enough for two people, as long as they curled up. It was not much of a shelter, but it was definitely better than being out in the open with the risk of exposure.

As nightfall came, we took turns using the sleeping bags. Everybody got a chance to sleep for a few hours before they were woken by the next users. I chose to stay up as long as possible as by then I was exhausted and knew I could sleep even in the cold. Those who were awake were expected to keep the fire going.

We were all expected to at least try and use the rifle. When it was my turn, the stock of the rifle slammed into my shoulder, leaving me with a large bruise. The rabbits we were supposed to shoot got a reprieve. The snares were set, but no animals were caught. Maybe if we had really been lost we would have tried harder. At least we knew the theory. In the afternoon of the second day, a vehicle came and picked us up. It was an interesting, as well as practical event and one I don't imagine too many people get to experience.

***

Flying in the North was always an adventure. The plane in Rae was a two-seat Cessna, and I had to sit in the luggage area so the patient would have the passenger seat. If the patient needed a stretcher or more room, a bigger plane was sent from Yellowknife.

The pilots were definitely a special kind of person. They were at times daredevils, but never took chances if patients were on board or we had to get out or back in a hurry. However, they did love to scare me if we had time and I was on my own returning to base from a few days in a community. If the pilot saw some caribou or another big animal, the plane would suddenly swoop down to have a look.

One day, when we had taken a patient to Yellowknife and were returning to Rae, we began circling a lake on the way. I didn't know what was happening. Carl, the pilot, was talking and talking on the radio phone, and we eventually landed on the lake on pontoons just missing some trees, or so it seemed to me. We had apparently been losing fuel.

A truck came to pick us up and take us back to Yellowknife. We were then given a lift back to Rae. I don't know how the plane was recovered, but eventually it reappeared in Rae, a few days later.

On another occasion with the same pilot, we returned to Rae from one of my fly-in communities. We landed on the lake and Carl shut off the engine, but before the plane could be tied up and we could disembark, the wind picked up. Before we knew what was happening, we were floating out into the middle of the lake. The people waiting for us thought it was very funny and much laughter was heard. Carl had to get out onto a pontoon and with an oar, paddled us back to shore. It took some time for the incident to be forgotten as we were teased by many of the onlookers.

Despite the antics at times, we learned to respect the pilots' judgements. They rarely took chances and it was often their word we took when deciding to fly or not. We had to rely on the opinion and knowledge of the pilot when deciding whether a patient could be safely transferred. Carl, in Rae, owned his plane and was therefore very protective of it. Not only was it his livelihood, but he loved to fly. He did, however, always take into account what we had to say about the urgency of the trip.

Once, I was asked to pick up a patient in Fort Simpson. We started off, but after some time, the fog came in, and we could see very little. Even with maps it was very difficult to make progress. Eventually, after circling for a while, the pilot spotted a river and followed it until the fog lifted a bit. We were then able to go on to our destination.

During the medevac flights we were in the air for various lengths of time and it was often cold. Once the patient was picked up and secured in a warm sleeping bag, we set off back to Yellowknife. If they happened to need an IV, it was often too cold for it to function properly. The bag was frequently placed beneath our parka to keep it warm and flowing as we stood over the patient, acting as a pole.

Occasionally, Public Health Nurses were asked to fly to Edmonton when a patient needed more specialized treatment. We were always pleased if the flight was nearer the end of the day as it meant a night in a hotel in Edmonton. As the patient was often more ill on these flights, the trip was not always easy, but a night away gave us some reprieve.

From time to time, we were stuck in Edmonton for a couple of days because there were no flights to Yellowknife. This meant that we had two days to wander about and, if possible, go to the West Edmonton Mall.

At first, we were booked into a hotel that was slightly off the main drag. This turned out to be a bit seedy. We soon discovered that it was a place where prostitutes worked. It was not unusual for doors to be knocked in the night with someone asking to be allowed in. Not the best situation.

Individually we documented this behaviour and finally the administration paid attention and we were moved to another hotel nearer the city centre from which we got a good night's sleep without harassment. When the staff of the clinic knew there was a medevac to Edmonton, a list was given to pick up certain articles that were unavailable in Yellowknife. Always on the list were Tim Horton's doughnuts.

Flying was something I had to do for the five years I was employed by the federal government. Once the Northwest Territories government took over health for the region it was decided that it would be more efficient to hire nurses that were designated to do the medevacs. We were quite relieved by this, as it allowed us to do the work for which we were trained without interruption. We did, however, continue to fly on occasion, as we were still expected to relieve nurses in the smaller communities when they were going on holiday.

University

During my years in NWT I enjoyed visiting my brother and sister-in-law in Victoria and had done so on many occasions. I liked to go in March, to celebrate birthdays and get some relief from the cold weather. I decided that my next move would be to Victoria, but this meant that, despite having twenty-three years of experience in nursing, I was required to also have a degree. When working in Newfoundland and NWT I had no problem having my qualifications accepted but British Columbia required that all nurses have a degree, especially if they were to work in the community.

On one of my trips south, I made an appointment at UVIC with a nursing professor to find out what I needed to do to be admitted to the programme. Lots of paperwork was needed, including references from Scotland. This correspondence took a great deal of time as it was done by snail mail back and forth over the Atlantic. As I had not been to school in Canada, I needed to prove that I could write English and pass a university course.

I returned to Yellowknife to start the next step in my life. At that time, a well-known pharmacy was opening in the area, and to celebrate, they had door prizes. Everybody was putting in their names and so did I. On the day the prizes were to be drawn, I learned that I had won the main prize, a computer.

It seemed as if it was a sign that I was making the right choice for my next step. There was no internet back then; however, it did allow me to type my papers to send them to Victoria.

I chose to do a course in sociology, which was provided by the Knowledge Network. I was sent a box with the book I needed to study and other papers I was required to read. I was also able to phone the professor, if needed. I wrote the papers and sent them to him. Eventually, they were returned with comments and marks. I found out that I had passed with an average mark, but it was good enough to start at university.

The Canadian Nurses Association gave scholarships every year, and I applied. I wrote a paper on working in the North as part of my application and sent it in. I heard back that I had won a scholarship of $2,000, which back then was a good sum.

In Yellowknife, once word went out that I was leaving to go to UVIC; one of the teachers in my high school asked me if I would like to rent her house. I immediately thought that it was a good idea, so agreed. With no internet, I was unable to find out easily if the rent was reasonable. I was just glad to have a place to stay. Back then, we were allowed to have our household effects moved by the government. As I had no furniture to move, I packed my car with everything I owned, and the car was moved to Victoria by long-distance transportation. I continued to drive that car for twenty-eight years before they were no longer being made and parts were too difficult to find.

The year before I went to university, my brother and sister-in-law moved to Nanaimo. This meant that I did not know anybody in the Victoria area, leaving me, yet again, in a place on my own, with a new adventure ahead.

I moved into the rental house and waited for my car to show up. The house had two bedrooms and a large basement.

There was a car in the garage under the main bedroom. My own car, therefore, stayed outside. All the space under the main floor meant that the rooms above were very cold. In the first few days, I explored the area and discovered the nearest grocery store. I had arrived at the end of August, with school beginning after the long weekend in September. Once the car was dropped off, I drove to the university to pick up a parking pass and get some idea of where the buildings I needed to access were.

I arrived at school on the day after Labour Day weekend and wondered why the car parks were quiet. Making my way to the nursing department, I met up with a few other people who were starting their nursing degree. We sat around talking, but after some time, we began to wonder why no classes were beginning. It turned out that classes did not start until later in the week. Obviously, university was going to be different than working in the community.

I settled in fairly quickly and soon found that I was not the only person starting university in their forties. The majority of the nursing students were already RNs, who had to now get a degree. We all had to study full time and yet many had children and also worked part time. They were a very hard-working group, who had little spare time as it was mostly work, school, and family. As a result, we probably had a very different experience than other, mostly younger, students.

I had applied for my Canadian citizenship before leaving Yellowknife. However I did not get notice that I had an appointment with a citizenship judge, to sit my test, until I arrived in Victoria. I had studied the questions for some time and felt confident that I knew the answers to any questions she would throw at me. I certainly felt I knew a lot about how the Canadian government worked.

I became a citizen at the beginning of November 1990, two months after starting at University, accompanied by three of my classmates. After the ceremony, we all went to the Empress Hotel for tea.

Sitting around in a classroom took some getting used to as I was usually on the go every day. I made sure that I went for a decent walk after lunch in the cafeteria. My treat, once a week, was a rice crispy square, which was so big that I made it last three days.

I soon got into the routine of studying, joining a couple of study groups to help me find out the best way to present papers. Once I caught on to what was expected, it got easier. Some courses were relatively easy, but others like statistics — which all students had to take — I found nearly impossible. After a few weeks, I went to the professor and asked for help. She was great and gave me extra time after class for further explanation. I managed a pass, but with little to spare. Math was never my strongpoint.

Whenever I needed a break from studying, I explored the area I lived in. This tended to happen on Fridays, during my first year, as I had no classes that day.

One memorable day, I took ten dollars and walked downtown. I was reasonably well-dressed and went to a few art galleries. In those days, coffee was provided to customers. From there, it was in and out of the many bookstores, where I picked up a second-hand book at a reduced price. It was then onto Chinatown for a late lunch, a walk around the harbour, and a visited to a couple more art galleries. On the way home, I passed a lottery booth. Not one for lottery tickets, I decided on a whim to by a Scratch 'N Win with my last dollar. Surprise, surprise . . . I won eight dollars, which meant that my day out, with coffee, lunch, a book and art viewing, cost me all of two dollars.

My mother had an elderly cousin who lived in Sidney; about twenty minutes drive from Victoria, at that time. At least once a month, on a Sunday, I would visit her in the afternoon. She loved to walk into town and have coffee at the local bakery. On occasion, she and I had supper at a restaurant on the waterfront. Mostly, however, she liked for me to make her poached eggs on toast.

Mum's cousin was able to fill me in on some of the family history. Married early in Scotland, she and her husband had come to Canada in their late teens. I never met her husband as he had died many years previously, but I had heard a great deal about him and his time in the Canadian Air Force. She was a great character, and I enjoyed our time together, as she had many stories to tell.

***

During my first winter in Victoria, the house was very cold, and I found myself spending more and more time in the university library just to keep warm for longer. I found some wool in a thrift store and crocheted myself a blanket to put over me when I studied or watched television. Then I would transfer it to the bed at night. It became so cold that I decided to invest in an electric blanket. From then on, I spent more time in bed, where I did much of my studying. It had been very different in the North as we were given a heating allowance, which meant my apartment there was always a comfortable temperature.

The first year passed quickly, and I found that I enjoyed studying and learning new ways of looking at topics. Many of the nursing topics were discussed at length, as many of the students had a great deal more knowledge about certain subjects than the professors. It was an intense year, as seven subjects had to be taken each term to allow us to complete the degree in two years.

As the year went on, I realized that my rent was much higher than the amount others in my class were paying. My landlady also expected me to cut the grass and keep the garden tidy. When she asked me to get the eaves cleaned, I found someone to do it. After I informed her, she told me it was too expensive, and proceeded to haggle over giving me my money back. I decided then that I had to find somewhere else to live. I made the decision to try and buy an apartment, as I had saved some of the money from selling my place in Scotland. I had also taken out the pension I had accumulated over the ten years I had worked in Canada. So, with that, my good credit rating, and the fact that I was going back to nursing, the bank gave me a mortgage, which covered my needs and allowed me to put in a minimum down payment.

I looked at many, many places before I came to the condo I finally bought. It was bright, had plenty of window space, and a long balcony. The area in the front was, at that time, called the Saanich slums, where there were many old run down houses, but there were enough trees outside my living room and bedrooms to partially camouflage the view. I continue to live there now, and since that time, the slums have been demolished, and a park has taken their place.

I was happy with my new home, but I had no furniture. My real estate broker was about to move in with his girlfriend and had a bed he no longer needed, so he kindly donated it to me.

My parents decided to visit that summer, making me scramble to find items to sit on and eat from. I quickly bought a futon using my student discount, which provided me with a seat and a bed, and a friend gave me an old table and two dining chairs. I set up a bookshelf made from bricks and boards, on which I put my tiny television and my books. I also had to rush out and get a few dishes, a couple of pots, and a kettle. I took the ferry over to Vancouver and picked the folks up at the airport, returning the same day. We settled into the sparse apartment, but as the weather was good every day, we were out more than in. I had already lined up a job in NWT before they came, so their time with me was limited. We made the most of it before I drove them to Nanaimo to finish their holiday with my brother. It turned out to be the last time they came together to Canada, making it a memorable holiday.

I had gone to NWT to work during my summer break, where I worked for eleven weeks straight. I made enough money to support myself for a few months, making it worth the long hours. It was good to return to a place of my own, however.

During my second year of university, we were allowed to pick two elective courses. I choose archeology and, later, international nursing. I also noticed that there was a massage course offered for students, but it was off campus. It was one evening a week, and a fellow student and I decided to take the six-week course, at a bargain price for students. We learned techniques, but best of all, we gave and received a massage each session.

Studying took up the majority of my time, and I was determined to do as well as I could. At one point, the nurses' marks were disputed by another faculty member as they were much higher than average. Our papers were sent to the University of Toronto for a second opinion. They were returned with the original marks upheld.

I enjoyed being a student and took advantage of all the benefits of my student card. One of these was tickets for the opera, as long as you were willing to sit in back of the theatre on the least popular night. I enjoyed several operas throughout the two years. I was also able to get my hair cut for a good price and have a coffee and a muffin in a local mall market for under a dollar.

Summer Work 1991

I needed to work during the summer at the end of my first university year. I phoned the office in Yellowknife to ask if there was any work available and was reassured they would need nurses all summer. I was flown up at the government's expense and driven out to Rae-Edzo the same community I had worked in several years previously.

The circumstances had changed. The cottage hospital in Edzo had closed not long after I left. My friend Barbara had been instrumental in transferring everything to Rae, where there was now a large clinic and a nurses' apartment block. I had visited her in her new accommodation on several occasions and was therefore familiar with the new situation. Barbara had moved on herself, a few months after setting everything up. I was given a well-stocked one-bedroom apartment where furniture, linen, and dishes were provided. Everything we needed was supplied, except for personal electronics. As a result, I brought with me my small radio for entertainment and to keep me up to date with world news.

While I was working in Rae that summer, I was also taking a course to make up my credits. The only phone that we were able to use for long distance calls was in the clinic. I wrote my papers and sent them to my professor at the University of Victoria. She, in turn, phoned me in the evening, about a week later, with her comments. This would have worked out well had the clinic phone not been in full view of the main door. I knew that if I put on the light someone would come to the door. To avoid being disturbed, I had to talk while sitting on the floor under the desk and take notes as best I could by the dwindling daylight

There were six other nurses when I arrived, but three were going on holiday a few days after my arrival. The Grey Nuns, whom I had known six years earlier, had all moved on. Now, only two replacement nuns were living in the small house designated for them next to the church.

I was assigned to work in the clinic, but also had the public health duties of pre- and postnatal care and immunizations. There had been a huge tuberculosis problem in the community a few years prior and over sixty cases needed constant follow-up, often at home.

After the three staff members left on holiday, four of us remained: me, two male nurses — Ian and John — and Mary, a fellow Scot, who had additional training as a midwife. I had worked with male nurses in psychiatry, but it was a new experience working with men in a clinic. We all worked well together, and I learned a great deal from everybody, especially the men, who had both worked in emergency units before coming north. Any time there was a new procedure that I had not done before, the "boys" called for me. They taught me and I learned a great deal from their knowledge.

We went about our daily tasks, with me in the clinic in the mornings and doing home visits, along with my new interpreter, in the afternoons. Unfortunately, the interpreter Mary Adele, whom I had worked with in Rae-Edzo before had died of cancer a couple of years earlier.

It all went well for a while. Soon, however, we began to realize that Mary had a problem with alcohol. She had managed to keep it under control when the head nurse was there, but now that Sister Cecile was on holiday, things changed. It was a dry community, meaning alcohol was only available when the bootleggers brought it in. Mary soon tracked down the alcohol source, and before long, we knew there was a problem developing. She being a fellow Scot somehow made it initially embarrassing. One night, after we had finished for the day, the noise coming from Mary's apartment just across the corridor from mine became unbearable. Mary had gone home, drunk a great deal, turned on her television and radio at full volume, opened all her faucets and switched on her vacuum cleaner. No matter how much we banged on the door, she did not stir. Fortunately, she was on the ground floor and John finally managed to pry open a window and let himself in. He found Mary passed out on her sofa. He let Ian and me in and we set about turning off the noise and trying to wake Mary. We finally managed to get her into bed and left her to sleep it off.

The drinking persisted, and on a day when she was needed, Mary did not turn up for work. A couple came in that day, and the woman was obviously in labour and needed help immediately. We knew that Mary would be no help. Both male nurses had never been to a birth, and therefore, it was up to me. I am not a midwife, but had safely helped deliver a baby some years previously, which gave me minimum confidence. With my heart in my mouth and the help of the other two nurses, we got her onto the bed so I could examine her. Already the head was beginning to crown, and as this was her third child, she fortunately knew about breathing and pushing. We were all very happy when Victoria was delivered without much trouble. The cord was cut, drops were put into the baby's eyes, and finally, the placenta came. We kept the mother and baby in for some time and they were, of course, visited by most of their relatives. We nurses could have done with a celebratory drink, but unfortunately it was still illegal.

On another occasion, I was woken in the middle of the night by John. A teenager had been badly beaten and raped. He had done what he could with the external wounds, but did not want to do the rape kit. Neither John, myself, or the RCMP officer who brought her in had done this procedure before. We undid the kit and read what to do. John and the officer stood at the head end of the examination table, while I took the swabs. Many swabs were needed, with each one bagged and labelled separately. This had to be done as quickly as possible after the event.

The RCMP officer read out what was needed and I, as gently as possible, carried out the instructions. Trying to remain professional was difficult under the circumstances. The girl had gone through a horrific experience, and it felt as if she was being exploited again. Unfortunately, to have proof of the culprit it was all necessary. After we finished the essential physical work and completed the obligatory paperwork, we manage to get her settled. John and I stayed with her until the ambulance from Yellowknife was able to travel to pick her up and transport her to a larger facility.

One night when I was on call, I was awakened by my beeper going off. I got up and went to the clinic to answer. A story emerged of someone being "very sick" in one of the homes. The person on the phone wanted me to go out and see the patient. I felt uncomfortable going out in the middle of the night as I did not know that particular family. I made the decision to go, but phoned the priest to ask if this was a sensible move. He spoke the language, having been in the community for over thirty years, and knew the families well. He agreed to come with me. I waited for him to get ready and together we walked over to the house. Many people were there and several had been drinking.

The bootleggers had obviously managed to avoid the police. The patient was in bed with a curtain around her. I managed to examine her and, with the priest's help translating, came to the conclusion that she had a fairly minor problem that could be helped quite easily. She was the elder in the household and had needed someone with authority to get everybody out. Father was the ideal person to persuade everybody to leave and allow her and her daughter to be left in peace and not be harassed by a group who were drunk.

In the middle of the night, later in the week, John came banging on my door. He needed help with a group of men who had arrived at the door of the clinic. They had been driving from Alberta, drinking on the way, and gone off the gravel road near the Rae road end. Somehow, they had managed to get themselves to clinic carrying one of the men, who was badly injured. The rest of the group also had many injuries. Fortunately, a doctor had been in the settlement for a few days, and she came as soon as she was called. The doctor, John, Ian, and I went about caring for these men. Although Mary was still in the community we did not call her as she was unpredictable. Each nurse took a patient, while the doctor went from one to the other to assess the problems. A nurse and the doctor worked on the man who had been carried in. It became apparent fairly soon that he had died. To keep the situation as calm as possible, we decided not to tell the other men about their friend until their own needs were assessed and treated. They continued to ask about their friend and became belligerent when we would not allow them to see him. We patched and sewed up several wounds, took X-rays, applied bandages, and generally cleaned the men up. Once the situation was clear, we decided to tell them about their friend's demise. They immediately went berserk. They pulled off bandages, threw chairs, and managed to hit nurses. One of us reached the phone and got through to the nearby RCMP station. After what seemed like forever, but was probably only a matter of minutes, three officers arrived with guns drawn. They brought order and escorted the four men to the police station, where they spent the night before being transferred to Yellowknife. The police inquiry started the following morning, and the body was removed. Fortunately, the staff only had minor cuts and bruises; however, it was a very scary episode.

Into the Unknown

On the road to Rae- Edzo. There were trees in the area, well beyond both each side of the road. An area on either side of the road was now filled with gravel.

* * *

An event I joined that summer took place at the grave yard. Once a year, in the summer, all the graves in the Rae cemetery were cleaned and the little fences around each grave repainted white. On the appointed Sunday, instead of people going to Mass as usual, the parishioners met at the graveyard, which was situated a little way out of town. I was included as part of the cleanup crew. Everybody participated, and within a few hours, the place looked neat and tidy. Once all the work was done, the priest performed Mass. I sat on a knoll and watched. After the service, fires were lit, food was produced from all kinds of carriers and spits were set up. After a while, we were all able to fill our plates with caribou, fish, and bannock, with tea to drink. A couple of the men took great delight when they ask me if I wanted to taste rat. The look on my face made them laugh heartily. It turned out to be muskrat, which I did try. It was a very dark meat that tasted a bit gamy, but it was worth trying. It was yet another type of food that I had tried and now added to my variety list.

I worked that summer for nine weeks straight in Rae until the regular staff returned. I discussed Mary's problem with the head nurse, as she obviously needed help. I have no idea if help was offered, or taken, as I was transferred to Fort Liard, where I had worked once before.

The first time I had been sent to work in Fort Liard it was in the winter, which meant a very different experience. This settlement was very dissimilar to Rae. They had quite a few shops there — including tourist-type places — as well as a café where a good coffee could be found. There were several private companies in Fort Liard, including an airline, where many local people were employed. The clinic was new and large, with the clinic itself on the ground floor and two nurses' apartments upstairs. On my previous visit, I had worked and lived in a trailer.

The other nurse, on this occasion was a man who lived with his wife, a teacher, in another part of town. This meant that I was first on call when anybody came to the clinic after hours or during the weekend. No cell phones in those days meant that I could not stray too far from the clinic.

Bert and I worked together at the clinic all day, and then he went home. One night, a loud knock at the door woke me. An RCMP member was brought in by a friend as he had fallen while playing basketball and hurt his leg. I had a look and decided that it was a two-nurse type of treatment. The leg was obviously broken, and as it was night time with no chance of getting him out to a larger city before the morning, it had to be dealt with as soon as possible. Bert arrived, and we worked together to X-ray and stabilize the leg, giving the patient medication to ease the pain in the process. We decided that a cast would be needed, and we set about gathering the materials. Neither of us had done this before, which added to the problem. With a lot of discussion, and a bit of trial and error, we successfully managed to manufacture a decent cast, which we were all pleased with. We kept the patient in overnight, and the next day, an RCMP plane came and picked him up. We heard later that he was progressing and that our cast had done a good job.

There were no more emergencies to deal with over the two weeks I was in Fort Liard. I had been to almost all provinces by that time and was looking forward to adding Yukon to my list, as it was only about a twenty-kilometre drive away. With no cell phone, however, I was unable to go on this trip. To this day, I have yet to go to the Yukon.

I returned to Yellowknife at the end of the two weeks for some R and R, where I looked after the house and the cats of friends, allowing them to go on holiday. I spent some time visiting old friends while I was there, but I definitely enjoyed a great deal of sleep.

Thailand

Before Christmas during our second year of university, a bunch of us were at one of the professor's homes for supper. During our discussion, we decided that the nursing department should branch out by doing something unique and innovative. Someone suggested an overseas trip, and Thailand was one of the countries on the list. Before the night was out, the professor was on the phone with the Dean, and our idea was proposed. As the weeks and months went on, the trip idea was developed and international nursing became a course. The idea was to do research about the country, its inhabitants, their health care and nursing education and present our findings to the class and other university faculty prior to going on the trip. We then attend lectures in Thailand given by nursing professors from two universities. One was in Khon Kaen and the other in Bangkok. In Thailand, health care was highly regarded as one of the kings family had been a nurse. At that time nurses were in charge of the many clinics found both in the cities and out in the more rural areas.

Twenty five of us flew to Hong Kong and stayed there for three days before going to Thailand where we were for three weeks. I was sharing a room with someone I did not know well, but we managed to make it work. In Hong Kong, we participated in a few organized trips, like sailing in a junk in the bay. We also visited the Aberdeen market and several other known areas of the city. On the third day, we could explore on our own. Four of us planned to continue with the holiday once the main trip was over, and we stayed together for much of the time. We made the most of our free time, taking a bus to the outskirts of the city, and visiting parks and markets.

In Bangkok, we were met by professors and other teaching staff from the city's university and then attended lectures. We also had lots of free time and took advantage of this by visiting many well-known tourist spots. We were taken around by bus on occasion.

On one of these outings, we stopped at a parking lot so people could use the washroom. We found a washroom that consisted of a hole in the ground. One by one, we went in and out, and just as the last person exited, a huge snake slithered out after her.

Another incident occurred when we took small boats up a river to visit a small remote community. On the way, the boat I was on got stuck on a sand bank. We all had to get out and push it free before getting on our way.

After our initial time in the city, we travelled to Khon Kaen where we again had lectures at the university. We were paired up with local nurses at this time, and I went out with one of the community nurses. She worked on her own and had a mostly rural area to cover. There were lots of houses on stilts to manoeuvre around, with evidence of poverty everywhere. In one village, there was a three-legged cow, fenced in, below the house. Despite its deformity, it was obviously a prize possession. Another place we visited was a hotel-like establishment, where I soon found out many prostitutes were housed. They had regular health checks and were treated for various ailments and sexually transmitted diseases, as needed. It was an eye opener to see just how young many of them looked. We also visited a few clinics run by nurses.

From Khon Kaen, we travelled back to Bangkok where we then flew to Chang Mai in the north, to visit the Golden Temple. That and many ruins were wonderful to see. Two other places we visited were a leper colony where people were treated, but lived in complete isolation, and a refugee camp where there were many children with their families living in huts.

We returned to Bangkok for final lectures. One evening, after being in the classroom a few of us were invited to the home of a young man one of the professors on the trip had befriended. Five of us accepted his invitation, and we had a very interesting time. Just before he opened the door to the kitchen area, he told us to be quiet. He then opened the door quickly to reveal dozens of geckos that scattered everywhere. He thought it was hilarious and enjoyed our reaction.

We moved from Bangkok to the coast and a resort to end the trip. We had a couple of days there to enjoy the amenities and eat great food. We were amazed by the artistry of the fruit that was cut into very intricate shapes.

It was time, then, for most of the group to return to Canada. Four of us had three more weeks planned and one other person was visiting a Thai friend. We said our farewells and then moved to a cheaper hotel in Bangkok. We spent a few days there, continuing to explore the city. One of the things we did was to have a manicure and pedicure. I have a photograph of us sitting on the side of the road showing off our red nails. We travelled by bus and ferry to Ko Samui, one of the islands. At the ferry terminal, we found many people advertising places to live. We chose one, after a bit of haggling, and piled into his van. It turned out to be a hut on the beach with an area nearby where the owner provided food. On our second day, we hired two motor bikes and toured the whole island. The very large Golden Buddha was well worth seeing. The owner of the place we were staying knew a lady who did Thai massage, and we all agreed to try a session. It turned out that the lady was quite elderly, but she gave each of us a terrific massage, for very little money. We ended up having one every day. To allow quiet during the massage, others were quite happy to swim and tan on the beach.

We returned to Bangkok and went to the bus station where we boarded a bus to Kuala Lumpur, in Malaysia. We found seats together and set off. On the way, one of us was reading a woman's magazine. A monk sitting near us pointed to the magazine, smiled, and indicated he would like to look at it. He definitely enjoyed looking at the photographs of more scantily clad women than he was used to observing. At the border, we showed our documents, and I was asked to get off the bus and go to the office. There, a very official man in uniform and broken English told me my documents were unacceptable. I was shocked, scared, and worried that the bus would take off without me. After a lot of talking between him and another man, who might have been in charge and spoke better English, I was let go and boarded the bus. It turned out that when my visa was stamped, it was slightly blurred and the dates were not clear.

When we arrived in Kuala Lumpur, we stayed with a nursing friend of one of the people on the trip. We slept on mattresses on the floor, and ate with the family. We spent time exploring the city and the neighbourhood where we were living. It became obvious immediately that it was a Muslim country. As I had not done much research into the country, I was quite surprised by the contrast with Thailand, which was mainly Buddhist.

One day, we took the train to Ipoh to visit the caves. On the way, a few ladies with babies asked us to hold their children. They seemed delighted that we held the babies and smiled a lot before taking them back. None of us were sure why this happened, but it was interesting. In Ipoh, we visited the caves, which are a well-known tourist attraction. We then had a meal with a couple who were friends of the family we were staying with in Kuala Lumpur.

Our Malaysian host family heard on the news that there had been riots happening in Thailand, so travelling back by bus was not possible. We managed eventually to get seats on a plane and returned to Bangkok. We landed and, as we stepped outside, were confronted with nearly empty streets. We managed to get a taxi to the hotel we had booked prior to travelling. Tension was felt as we made our way back to the city. Once back at the hotel, we managed to contact one of the professors we had gotten to know at Bangkok University. The next day, she picked us up and took us to one of the hospitals. The wards were full to overflowing as most people had stayed home when the riots were taking place, as there had been shooting on the streets. We helped in the maternity ward, mainly pushing beds around. Two of our group were midwives and were able to do a little more, but without the language it was difficult. The queen of the country took a special interest in health and childbirth was given a pride of place at the hospital. It was interesting to find that music was played several times a day, and the patients were expected to do exercises while lying on their beds during that time. We were taken out for lunch by some of the nurses. They had a great time tempting us to try various foods. It caused great hilarity when a very hot pepper sauce was tasted and resulted in the typical facial expressions and grabbing of water. We did learn that taking a spoonful of rice helped to cool down the mouth.

We were on our feet all day in great heat. When we finally reached the hotel in the evening, my feet were like balloons. I had to sleep with my feet and legs placed up the wall. In the morning, I was back to normal.

One thing we were taught by the professor was how to sit if we were ever to meet the king. Why we needed to know this was a mystery, but she had fun teaching us.

We met up with the nurse who had been staying with her friend in Bangkok at the airport on our way back to Canada. She had been scared as there had been quite a bit of violence with a lot of noise during the riots and one tourist from New Zealand had been shot. We were obviously protected from it all and oblivious to the dangers. Victoria University had been trying to contact us as they heard about the riots before we were aware of them. Nobody had cell phones back then, so we could not be contacted.

Our journey back was uneventful. We were met at the airport by some rather worried staff and friends. We had a wonderful trip with a great deal of variety in the places we visited, the food we ate, and the situations we encountered. Mixing academic learning, some practical insight, and tourism was an ideal way of travelling and seeing a country in a different way. This was something I was to repeat some years later.

Return to University

Our final papers for university were written in Thailand, and the professor marked them on the way home. I believe that everybody did well. It was the last of the work we had to complete before finishing our degrees. On my return, however, I learned that, as I had not sat an official UVIC English exam, I could not get my degree. After two years of full-time studying and having written many, many papers and exams, I was shocked. I believed that I had passed an entrance English test when I was admitted two years prior. Until that time, I had not been questioned concerning any missing credits. After some manoeuvring and sending in my best paper — which was my only A plus — to two professors from different faculties, it was agreed that my English was acceptable. Once that problem was fixed, I was granted my degree.

We prepared for convocation by getting photographs done with gowns. It turned out that the photographer did not know the correct way to put on the hood, which for nursing was peach coloured. We ended up with a unique photograph, as our hoods were lower than they should have been.

Three of us had gone to Vancouver prior to the trip to Thailand. During that weekend, we went to several jewellers on Granville Island and finally chose a pattern to have a special ring made for our class. It had a whale and the healing hand for nursing. Many in the class ordered them either in gold or silver. Mine was silver, to match the ring the nuns had given me. I continue to wear both today.

Convocation day came, and it was quite exciting. We dressed in our gowns, wore the hoods properly with our mortarboards, and met outside the auditorium. One by one, we piled into the seats assigned to us.

My brother, sister-in-law, and a friend were in the audience. Once the speeches were over, it was our turn to receive our degrees. I had bought a pair of shoes with heels for the occasion, while I had been in Bangkok. My feet are small and getting heels in Canada is nearly impossible. Not used to wearing anything but flats, I walked warily over the stage to kneel before the chancellor. My tassel was turned, and I was given the degree. I have to admit I was pretty pleased. I thought of my Grade Seven teacher, who when we were sitting our eleven plus exams in our last year of primary school, had told my mother not to put me down for high school, as he thought I would never make it.

After the ceremony and class pictures, we all separated to spend time with family and guests. My guests and I went down to Chinatown for a good Chinese meal. The next day, some of us from class met at a local hotel for brunch. My brother and sister-in-law accompanied me. This was the last time I saw the majority of my classmates, as we scattered all over the province. A few of us went, a few days later, to a wedding held in the university chapel and then the faculty club. The woman getting married was one of the ladies who had attended my citizenship ceremony.

***

The whole experience at university was memorable and one I would not have missed. I learned new ways of thinking about topics and despite my problems with statistics; I at least had a basic idea about how to look at charts and stats. I am not sure how much having a degree changed my nursing practice, but the experience gave me a confidence I had lacked before. I had enjoyed the course in Thailand and learned more than before about the Indigenous people from the area around Victoria by looking at local archeological sites during my elective course. I had bought a condo and knew that I would be staying in Victoria.

I decided to go home to Scotland for a long holiday prior to returning to work. Before setting off for six weeks, I sent out at least a dozen résumés. As there were no plants or pets to make arrangements for, I was able to leave my apartment and set off for my longer than usual trip.

In Scotland I stayed with my parents and visited family and friends. We went on several outings to Glasgow and climbed Tinto Hill, the highest hill in the area. We also took a trip to the Isle of Mull and Iona. We drove to Lincoln, in England, to visit my father's youngest brother and his wife. On the way during both trips, we stopped at many historic sites. By that time, my parents had moved to a cottage in a village near where Mum had enjoyed many happy times. It was also near where they had met while visiting their respective families during holidays as children. We explored the area, and I got to know the places they often talked about.

I returned to Victoria thinking that with my nursing experience, and a degree, I would have no problem finding work. I was wrong! I had no response from any of my resumés. I had some money to buy food and pay my monthly mortgage, but not much else, so getting a job was essential. I went to the health department and got a list of health centres throughout British Columbia. I phoned one after the other without much success.

Eventually, and with a great deal of persistence, I got the news from someone in Prince Rupert that they needed someone to cover maternity leave in Quesnel. I had no clue where it was, so I went to the library to look at maps. Once that was established, I phoned the health centre there and spoke to the nursing officer. After a telephone interview, I was given the job, which was to last four months.

I had made contact with a girl, who was a relative of someone I met at university and was heavily pregnant and needed a place to live. It was decided that she would live in my apartment until she had the baby. Our arrangement was that she pay for utilities and general upkeep. With this settled, I packed the car with the things I thought I might need and set off into another unknown.

Quesnel

The long journey to Quesnel started with the drive out to Swartz Bay, to catch the ferry; from there I found the way to Hope, and then drove up the Fraser Canyon. It seemed never ending, and I began to realize the vastness of British Columbia. It was quite the journey and one I got to know well over the years. In Quesnel, I met the nursing officer and then booked myself into a hotel for the night. I soon realized that I was going to have to find my own accommodation. I foolishly assumed that it would be provided, as it had been for the ten years I had so far worked in Canada.

After a few nights in the hotel, one of the nurses in the hospital offered me the use of her basement room until I found a place of my own. It had a bed and a room with a sauna. We had to schedule times for the use of the sauna as the shower was in the same room. I stayed with her for a month as I was lucky to find a one-bedroom apartment for rent near the centre of town. There was no furniture, but I borrowed a camping foamy to sleep on, and the family I had stayed with gave me a chair they no longer needed. I also needed a few kitchen items, which I found in various places.

My Apartment on a Sunday afternoon

Sunlight filtering in an amber splash
on a worn mustard carpet,
there is a timelessness in this room,
who has lived here,
loved here,
one can only speculate.

The public health office was a separate office building with offices, a reception area, clinic rooms, and a large room upstairs. Downstairs, we had our own offices, a small kitchen area with a sink and kettle, and a large meeting room. I shared an office with one other nurse, who worked part-time, allowing me some time alone. We also had two government cars kept in the car park behind the building, which we shared.

Public health office, rear view. The office was on the main street in Quesnel and near the hospital. The provincial cars were kept in the car park.

I soon learned that the areas I was given to cover were called West Quesnel and Narcosli, the latter being out of town and consisted mostly of ranches, but also included a one-room school. I had two elementary schools to visit in West Quesnel, plus one high school. In all, it was a big geographical area with some paved roads, but also some gravel roads.

It became apparent that the nurse on maternity leave was going to need more time off as her baby had problems and required a great deal of special attention. She decided to resign instead, and I applied for the job. I drove to Prince George for an interview, which I found a bit intimidating as I had never previously gone through one in Canada. I nevertheless got the job and decided to give Quesnel a year.

The majority of my clients in town were of East Indian origin. They had come to Quesnel to work in the many mills in town. This was a new experience for me and another ethnic community I had to get to know. I had always travelled a lot, and finding out about new communities and their views was something that had fascinated me for years. As new babies were born, I made home visits; it was a great way to get to know families and for them to get to know me.

The other nurses in the office were married and had their own lives. This meant that I spent most of my time off by myself. I settled into a routine of work with coffee on Saturday mornings in a local café where they had newspapers to read and did not seem to mind me doing the crossword. Once I found the library, I had plenty of books to read. I spent the rest of my weekends walking all over the town to find out what was available. I found a path along both the Fraser and the Quesnel rivers, which I walked along regularly. I discovered that many East Indian ladies also enjoyed these routes, and we smiled and nodded at each other. Evidence of beavers was present along the river, although I never did see one, just the gnawed trees and the piles of branches stretching over the water.

I enjoyed working in the primary schools I had, but the high school was another matter. Teaching school classes was never something I liked, as we seemed to have to teach the subjects that caused problems for the teachers. Sex education comes to mind, mainly with Grade Seven. Those students often believed they knew all the answers. Small, more intimate classes — like prenatal classes, or with a group who had a specialized topic to discuss — was more to my liking. It did need to be done, however, and I put effort into fulfilling the curriculum.

After a few months, I discovered that there was a small group of women who sang together on a regular basis. The community choir practised in the church near my apartment, and I joined them once a week. I was pleased to find a singing group as I had had sung when it was available in other places I had lived. We not only sang together, but socialized by meeting at each other's homes. We did not put on concerts, but sang at events in the town and in the church in Barkerville — a historic tourist town about an hour's drive away — at Christmas time.

I was just beginning to settle into Quesnel life when I got a phone call one evening to say that my parents had been in a road accident in England. My mother had been killed, and my father was in intensive care. I phoned the friend that I had had supper with, and she came to be with me and make arrangements for my flight to Britain.

Coordinating with my brother and sister-in-law who lived in Nanaimo was necessary. The three of us met at Vancouver airport and flew out to Manchester the same day. We had to buy an open-ended ticket as we had no idea what to expect. An uncle picked us up and took us to a hotel to rest before taking us to see Dad, who was in the ICU in Middlesburgh Infirmary. We visited the hospital for hours each day, after being told that his chances of survival were maybe fifty-fifty. We knew we were in for the long haul and decided to change lodgings to a pub with upstairs rooms, as it was less expensive. It was also much nearer the hospital and easier to walk to daily, and we were able to get pub food.

Two of my uncles in Scotland took on my mother's funeral arrangements, which was a great relief to my brother and me as doing this long distance was nearly impossible. They came to Middlesburgh to discuss the final details and for our input. My brother and sister-in-law went up to Scotland three days before the funeral, and I stayed on to be with Dad as long as possible. I travelled to Scotland by train the day before the ceremony, and we all stayed with an uncle and aunt.

The funeral at the crematorium was large as my parents were members of several groups, and many people from their village and from Dad's previous work place attended. Immediately after the ceremony, my sister-in-law returned to Canada, and my brother and I were driven back to Middlesburgh and the hospital.

Dad eventually came out of the ICU and into a ward. After several days, we were able to persuade the staff that returning to Scotland would make our life much easier and maybe help Dad's recovery, as he could have visitors. Eventually he was taken up in an ambulance to the nearest hospital to his home, and we returned by train. We continued the daily visits and were able to live in the family home. Bit by bit, Dad recovered, but we needed to stay for three months in the end. His freezer was filled up with as much food as we could produce, and we made sure that he was able to cook a variety of food before we left. I made lists of all the bills he had to pay monthly and what was needed for the bank as Mum had done all this work previously. Satisfied that he was going to cope and that he was fit enough to be on his own, we travelled back to Canada.

I was very surprised to find my boss waiting for me at the airport in Quesnel. I soon found out the reason. She drove me straight to work at one of the schools where all the nurses were doing a prekindergarten clinic. Without even taking my suitcase home, I was back at work, this despite having flown all night from Scotland to Vancouver and then taking another flight to Quesnel. I got the impression that taking three months off was not appreciated, despite the reason. From that moment on, the relationship with my boss deteriorated. She and I worked in very different ways. She was more of a "by the book" person, while I preferred to deal with every situation as it came.

All the nurses had to do their regular work as well as take on extra tasks. I chose to do a travel clinic, which took place every week. I loved finding out where people were going and joined in the excitement of them describing what they were expecting on their trip. We worked out what vaccines they needed and planned the vaccine schedule. Often, they returned to clinic to let me know how their trip had gone. Many people were going to India, and when bubonic plague developed in certain areas of that country, we had to make a special effort to contact people who were planning to travel there.

I discussed with several members of the East Indian community the best way to get information out to their population. It was agreed that I speak at the temple about this subject and one Sunday arrived to fulfill this task. I had never been in the temple, so was given a borrowed scarf to cover my head. I had to stand at the front of the main room and talk about the disease and what was necessary before travelling. I then sat on the floor at the back while the rest of the service continued. After that experience, I was invited to the temple on several occasions, but never had to speak again.

I enjoyed learning about the Punjabi way of life, as most of my clients were from that area in India. I eventually taught an ESL class, at the community centre, about health topics. Only women attended these classes, which were fun and included lots of laughs. During one of these classes, it became apparent that some of the ladies had never been to the clinic as they were a bit scared to go on their own. I suggested that I meet them one day and show them around. They came, and we sat in the big room downstairs where I explained how the clinic worked and what was available there. The boss appeared at the door and called me over to speak to her. She was not too pleased that I had invited people to the building without letting her know.

I attended many events at my clients' homes, including dinners, where I was introduced to food that I had not tried before. There were ladies' nights in a hall, with everybody dressed in their best, most colourful attire. I was given a typical salwar outfit to wear on these occasions. We had a lot of fun dancing and eating great food. In homes with new babies, the birth was always celebrated with food, and I was expected to eat something when visiting. I have never liked tea with milk, so eventually word went out that the nurse had to have black tea instead of chai.

The area I had outside Quesnel was quite a drive, mostly on gravel roads. I was fortunate to be able to borrow one of the government vehicles — a 4-wheel drive, which was ideal in bad weather conditions — as long as care was taken. To get to Narcosli, I had to drive on a road that ran along a gully. I learned that a few years later, the road had collapsed and disappeared.

I travelled to the one-room school in Narcosli once a month, unless there was something particular to attend. Teaching these kids was interesting as they were many ages and at different stages of learning.

During my second year of working in the area, one the nurses, who with her husband had befriended me, decided to retire. She was replaced by two new grads. One originally came from Quesnel, and the other was from Vancouver. This changed the dynamics of the office. One benefit for me was that I was able to transfer the high school to one of the new nurses. I continued with my three elementary schools.

Extra Activities

At some point over this period, I became aware of classes in Prince George on Healing Touch. I had learned a little about Qigong in Yellowknife and had been intrigued with energy work ever since. I signed up, booked a hotel room, and attended my first weekend class. This was the start of a long training and of a great friendship.

During the first class, I worked with a woman who lived in Prince George. She invited me to stay with her whenever I attended future classes, as she had a three-bedroom home and lived alone. From then on, I stayed with her when I went to Prince George, and we became good friends. I often visited my friend between classes, too. During that time, we were able to practise what we were learning.

I continued to train in Healing Touch in Prince George on weekends, sitting the exams as I went. Once I felt confident that I could teach other people, I set up a workshop of my own using the facilities at the Quesnel Woman's Resource Centre. I was able to use the large room and the kitchen and asked all the participants to either bring a bath towel or a mat to lie on. I brought my massage table to the centre so I could teach the techniques. These workshop days became quite popular, and in the end, I put on several. From these, I began to have people come to my apartment for treatment, some on a regular basis. It was easy to put my foamy up against the wall of the bedroom to accommodate the massage table. As part of my training, I needed to treat and write up 100 cases. This I manage to do over a couple of years.

Unless I was in Prince George, I spent most of my weekends alone. I continued to draw, which I had been doing most of my life, and began to try my hand at poetry. My poetry was probably not the greatest, but it was something to think about, and it kept me busy.

> Quesnel hovers in black and white,
> Colour percolates in patches,
> Red a pale baby pink
> Blue a murky sky,
> In flashes ochre, cadmium, burnt umber,
> I wait for the day of vermilion and cobalt blue,
> For now Quesnel remains positive, negative,
>   black, white.

The year after the death of my mother, Dad decided to come to Canada for a holiday. He came for six weeks, spending the first two weeks in Nanaimo with my brother and sister in law, then coming to Quesnel for three weeks. We drove back together to Nanaimo for his final week. This became an annual event until he no longer could manage the journey. I bought a second-hand two-seat sofa bed to make his stay more comfortable.

On Dad's first trip to Quesnel I drove to Vancouver Island to pick him up, and we travelled back to Quesnel. I continued to work and, he found things to do around town. We always went to Prince George on the weekends to visit my friend.

One of the workers at the clinic, and her partner, befriended Dad, and he went out at least one evening a week to their place or out for an ice cream. My now-retired nursing friend, and her husband, had us for supper or a BBQ on several occasions. We drove back to Nanaimo for some family time and to celebrate Father's Day — always with a DQ ice-cream cake — before he went home.

Dad managed to travel by bus from Vancouver to Quesnel eventually, making it easier for me. It also allowed me to save more holiday time, part of which would have been taken up with driving. His visits continued for five more years. Once he was unable to travel alone, I went to Scotland every year to visit him.

***

I found out that the nursing department at the University of Victoria was planning a trip to China the following spring 1996, as a former student I could sign up and looked forward to exploring a new country. Later in the year, I got a phone call to say that several professors had dropped out, leaving only one going on the trip. I was asked if I would take on the duties of administrator while travelling, for which I would be paid some money. It was not enough to pay for the trip, but it helped. I did have to agree to share a room with the professor, however. She had taught me in the past, and did have a bit of a reputation, so I was a bit dubious. In the end, we worked together well, and the trip was successful.

In China, we started our trip in Shanghai and ended in Beijing. During our time there, we visited several health facilities, including a traditional Chinese medicine hospital, which was enormous. We also went to a herb farm where many medicines were grown.

We flew to Suzhou to attend a graduation ceremony, as well as some lectures from some of the university professors. On the flight we discovered that not all seats on the plane had seat belts. The ceremony was fascinating as many of the women in attendance were dressed in military uniforms. We were never told who the women in uniform were or why they were there. The nurses all stood while the military sat. Each graduating nurse received her certificate one at a time. During most of the ceremony there was very little noise, with the exception of a couple of speeches. Once the main event was over, the women in uniform left, and the atmosphere changed. Loud music started and everybody, including twenty of us, got up and danced. We also enjoyed some finger food. We discovered later that these nurses, all women, had no choice as to where they would be working as they were posted to where they were needed most.

We later went to Xian to see the Terra Cotta warriors. We also saw many other tourist attractions, including the Great Wall. In one city, the professor and I went for a walk in the area of the hotel. We thought we knew how to get back, but we were eventually lost. We decided to go into a police station for help, and eventually, our tour director came to our rescue. When we got back to the hotel, the students were sitting along the corridor waiting for us. It took a long time to live the event down.

Overall, it was great trip. We were able to go to places most tourists would not have been interested in or taken to, but we also saw many of the places that are so well known and not to be missed. China has changed a great deal since then, which makes the trip even more memorable.

The Fraser River walk, I walked here on a regular basis most often on a Sunday afternoon. It was not too far from my apartment.

After my trip to China, it was back to Quesnel and back to the routine of work. Sometime during my second year there, I was involved in setting up a conference on multiculturalism with a social worker and two nurses from the hospital. At this time, there was a debate in Canada about the RCMP wearing turbans. The officer involved lived in Quesnel and was one of the dads I visited. As a result, I knew about the animosity he and his family were facing.

The RCMP officer's sister was one of the nurses involved in organizing the conference. We planned a day with a speaker and then broke into discussion groups. We worked with the Women's Resource Centre and the college to get the word out. As the two nurses were from the Punjab area of India, we had a big response from that community.

One of my jobs as a coordinator for the conference was to make the posters. In the end, I decided to write this:

Cultures

Cultures like colours become more interesting when they mix.
Like colours cultures become more interesting when they mix
When they mix like colours cultures become more interesting.

The event was very successful and gave many of the participants a place to meet others and explore their respective ways of life. Everybody got a chance to speak if they wanted to, in the small groups. We had food provided by several people, who brought in their specialties. In that way, we had a great variety of mostly Western and Indian cuisine. The debate over turbans in the RCMP was eventually resolved.

Another conference I was involved in had to do with women's health. Several nurses from the hospital, as well as teachers from the college got together to sponsor the arrival of a well-known endocrinologist and woman's health expert from Vancouver. We put on a one-day event, with the endocrinologist as the main speaker. We also had a panel that consisted of one of the local GPs, some nurses, and a social worker. I was also on the panel to speak about Healing Touch.

On the evening before the conference, I picked up the main speaker from the airport, and then we had a meeting with most of the local doctors in the town. It became quite a debate, as most of the doctors were men who had to be persuaded about certain aspects of women's health.

The conference was very well attended and had a very diverse audience. The morning was taken up by speeches from the panel, while much of the afternoon consisted of a question-and-answer session. This lasted longer than planned and could have lasted longer. It appeared that interest in this topic was high and that many questions still needed to be answered. I took the main speaker to the home of a friend for supper and then to her hotel. The next morning, I dropped her off at the airport. It had been a successful couple of days.

***

Quesnel had a lot of theatre — mostly amateur — and several times a year, musicians were invited to perform in the gym of the largest high school. Many were well-known performers. So I kept myself busy, attending those performances, having meals at a friend's home, learning to use a lathe, exploring the area, singing, and doing Healing Touch.

I did, however, have some time free and decided to teach English to people who had problems with reading and writing. I took Project Literacy classes at the local community college and after getting the certificate, began to teach. I used to meet my students at the college in the evenings on a one-on-one basis. My first student was a lady who, despite having gone through the Canadian education system, had difficulties. After assessing her needs, we went through some basic learning. Eventually, it became apparent that what she really wanted to be able to do was read recipes. The reading and writing sessions changed then to include this aspect of her needs.

Another student had just divorced, and as his ex-wife had done all the banking, he was at a loss. We did some basic work and then concentrated on cheques and banking. At one point, we could not use the classroom in the college so we met at my apartment. I had no table, so he made me a fold-up table that I still have today. Several other students were Indian ladies who had come straight from India after marriage.

***

Over the years of working in Quesnel, there were little things that niggled at the relationship between my boss and me. I knew that if she came into my office and shut the door, it was not a good sign. Once, when the Minister of Health was visiting, I just happened to be near the bottom door of the building where the car park was situated. The minister decided to come in through there instead of through the main door, where she was expected and where the boss was waiting. I brought her in to a rather cold look and heard about it later, despite me having no part in the decision taken.

I passed all my Healing Touch exams and went to Vancouver to get my certificate and pin. I was lucky enough to have the president, who had come up to Canada from Denver, present the new practitioners at the ceremony. On my return to

Quesnel, I decided to write my new achievement as a certified Healing Touch practitioner (CHTP) on the card we left at homes when there was no answer. The boss found out and was furious, demanding that I take it off immediately.

A new nurse was hired, and as she did not have an office, a wall was built to partition off the large meeting room and provide her with space. It was a plain white wall where I decided some art was needed. One weekend, I went to the office and put up some drawings of Quesnel that I had done over the years. The next morning, as the nurses came in, they were quite intrigued by the drawings and seemed to enjoy them. The boss, however, told me to take them down immediately and not to think about putting anything else up. After that, I gave my situation a great deal of thought and assessed the need to continue under the circumstances.

New Directions

I walk quietly in the wind
my mind drifting in new directions
the sculptured trees
with wind- pruned symmetry
allows the imagination to grow roots
branches reach outward,
    skyward,
a tree rooted,
    myself searching
for shapes, for ideas, for promises.

A view of the river walk along the Quesnel River. This was a very popular trail which followed the river edge.

Not long after the incident with my boss about the drawings in the office, two things happened, one after the other. I had my fiftieth birthday, and for a laugh, I put some purple Kool-Aid in my hair to give me a streak. This was long before dying hair with wild colours became popular. On arriving at work, the boss sent me home to wash it out as she deemed it unprofessional.

The last straw for me, however, was when I followed a teenage single mother — whom I had been looking for, for quite some time — into the local mall. Someone reported that I had been seen in the coffee shop where I had taken her to talk. I was reamed out once again, and the next day, I handed in my notice.

Apart from my trip to China, I had taken no extensive holidays over the years. Dad had been coming to Canada, so I had not needed to go to Scotland. As a result, I had saved from my wages and was able to pay off my mortgage. Without a job, I packed up and returned to Victoria.

Victoria Again

After six years of living in Quesnel, I finally returned to Victoria. My apartment was thankfully empty as the girl who had been living there for all six years, had moved out to a place of her own. It had not been a formal rental but we had an arrangement that suited us both. It had been well looked after in my absence, and she had put in another bed, as her child had wet mine.

I had no job, but thought that I might earn some money by using my Healing Touch knowledge. I had some business cards made and left them in places I thought might attract customers. Fairly soon, I realized that having people I did not know in my home was probably not a good idea. Also, having clients without insurance or a business licence was not something I had thought about too closely. This idea was therefore dropped.

One day, I was wandering around downtown when I bumped into the professor I had met for my first interview, prior to getting into UVIC. She was also the person who led our trip to Thailand. She asked me what I was doing and then offered me a job at the university, as she had just been given a large grant and needed a research assistant. It was a big change for me and a huge drop in wages. It did, however, sound intriguing, and a job was a job.

Into the Unknown

I applied, completed the paperwork, and began what amounted to three years of work. Nurses need to have a certain amount of working hours to retain their licence, on a yearly basis, but as I was working in the nursing department at the university, I was able to count the hours there as research. I worked firstly on a project called AIMnet, where we were looking at how to prevent falls among the elderly. I spent most of my time in the library looking for articles that were relevant to the topic. At that time, we could look for papers on the computer, but not order them. I became very familiar with the stacks in the library. A student doing her PhD joined the group, and another person, who worked mainly on the computer, also joined. I became the generalist who did any job needed. This entailed mostly working in the library. On occasion, I picked up a grandchild from school.

We became involved in several seniors' homes throughout greater Victoria. There we observed the living areas, noting where the hazards might be for falls. A tick sheet was developed to help us record our observations. I spent many weeks in these homes, just observing. At first, the residents and staff where a bit wary of why I was there, but over time, I was ignored and allowed to get the work done.

Another plan that was put into action was getting municipalities to spray orange paint on cracks in the sidewalks, to make them more visible and prevent falls.

I accompanied the PhD student to the towns of Sechelt and Gibsons on the Sunshine Coast, in BC, to allow her to give a lecture at a workshop for a group of health professionals. It had been organized by our office and a public health officer from the coast. The student insisted we fly over to save time, even though we were staying for a couple of days. This was when I started noticing just how privileged professors and other teaching staff were. Over time, I became aware of how prevalent waste was at the university.

During the year, we put on a conference in which we invited speakers from all over Canada and two from the US. This cost a lot of money and took a great deal of planning. The speakers not only insisted on being paid the going rate, but expected to be put up in the best hotels in town and given incentives.

I missed all the benefits of my student days and now had to pay full price for everything. Living frugally had not been a problem, but suddenly I had to be very aware of every cent. Little things became important, and I took advantage of coupons and sales. I also enjoyed walks in nature, particularly the surrounding parks. I only used the car for work. I ate well, however, making a variety of healthy soups and stews. I also kept up my art practice by using what was available, for as little money as possible.

Dad continued to visit for six weeks in the late spring and got used to entertaining himself during the days I worked. He loved to go to the nearby Italian bakery and buy a box of very sweet cakes. Several friends took him out when they were free. He went up on the train to Nanaimo to visit my brother on a couple of occasions, and together we drove there for various celebrations. We always got together for Father's Day in Nanaimo with my sister-in-law's dad — where we celebrated with a meal and the expected ice-cream cake — before Dad went back to Scotland.

I continued to tutor English with Project Literacy in my spare time. I met my clients at the office a couple of hours a week. One of the students had joined the Mormon Church, and he needed to be able to read their Book of Mormon. After looking at it with him, it became apparent that it was far too difficult for his level. His second choice of subject was cars, so we, to my relief, immersed ourselves in that much easier topic. Another student had a mental handicap and wanted to read about the Olsen twins during every session. A third was from Italy and although her English was fairly good, she wanted to improve enough to get a job. We did a lot of talking while walking around various areas of the city.

At the end of the AIMnet project, I managed to find work with several professors before being hired as part of a team looking at making the Quadra area of Victoria into a more village-like atmosphere. We did extensive interviews with dozens of people who lived in the vicinity. Eventually, I worked exclusively in the office helping to collate the information coming in from the interviews. Several requests and needs emerged, but the most important was that a food store or supermarket came to the community. One did eventually relocate and appeared to give new life to the area, promoting further development.

***

Soon after I returned to Victoria I discovered that there was a Healing Touch group in town, and I made contact to keep up my practice. We got together every second week to have a practice session. With one of the other certified practitioners, we held two weekend workshops where students learned the basic concepts of the technique.

Another activity we provided was to offer treatments in the meeting room of a large downtown church. Tables were set up, and we managed to buy six foam mattresses to put on top. At first, it was mostly members of the church who came, but later quite a few street people turned up. Often, they were very pleased with the work done and at least two told me that they had not been treated or touched so gently for a very long time. We continued with this work for many months, however, eventually, the space was needed for other things. We donated the mattresses to a local charity that housed the street population. At these sessions, I met an elderly lady who had been a reflexologist for many years. I began to have treatments by her and decided to pursue this modality. I went to Vancouver for training on the weekends, over a period of several months. I was able to find a mentor in Victoria who observed my practice until I was certified. I have used the knowledge since.

Work at the university became more and more difficult to find, and I needed a job that paid me enough to live on. Fortunately, a friend noticed an advert in the local paper for a job as a public health nurse with the Inter Tribal Health Authority. They were looking for a nurse to work in the two local reservations in the Victoria area. I applied and went to Nanaimo for my interview. After a few days, I was informed that I had the job and prepared myself to working part time in another situation. It could not have happened at a better time as my final cheque from the university was for thirty-seven dollars.

Inter Tribal Health Authority

I started work in February 2002 with Inter Tribal Health becoming the nurse for Songhees and Esquimalt Nations which were near each other and about a twenty minute drive from my home. ITHA had its headquarters in Nanaimo and administered many small indigenous communities all over Vancouver Island. All of the nurses with the Inter Tribal Health Authority (ITHA) worked part time for a lot less money than nurses working in provincial public health. There were also no benefits or a pension. We did, however, get two extra weeks holiday at Christmas, as most band offices shut down over the celebrations. Still, I was glad to be back working in the area I was trained for and enjoyed.

Though I spent most of my time in the communities I was assigned, we had regular meetings at the ITHA main office, which was about an hour and a half drive from Victoria. Nurses' meetings were separate, but on occasion, the whole staff met. As the meetings started at 9:00 a.m., a very early start was needed to get there on time, especially in the winter. We had one nurse in charge, and she had an office in Nanaimo. During the eight years I worked for that employer, we had six nurses-in-charge. Every one of them had their own ideas about how the department should be run, and therefore, the rules and expectations changed on a fairly regular basis.

Each year, the nursing staff was invited to attend the federal nurse's conference in Vancouver. These occurred over a period of a few days. It was always good to meet others in the profession and see, in person, the people at the top who were making and changing the rules, and running the health services. It was also lovely to have a few days in a nice hotel with breakfast and snacks provided.

ITHA also had staff retreats where all the staff attended. We all went to a First Nation lodge on Quadra Island once, and the nursing staff returned again one other time. We also had other retreats in various places.

***

I had wrongly assumed that my experience working in the North with the Dogrib people would give me an advantage on the reserves. In NWT, however, there were no reserves, so this was a very different situation for me.

In the North, I had had an interpreter with me from the beginning. They had taken me around and introduced me to families. Everybody in my new places of work spoke English, so interpreting was not a problem, however no one in my new situation offered the same introductions, and I was left to find my own way. Every day, I worked by walking around in the community, hoping that someone would acknowledge me. It did not happen in either community for a very long time.

I discovered much later that there had been so many nurses in my job who had come and left, that people were no longer prepared to get to know me, as they thought I would leave quickly. Little did they know that a stubborn Scot was their new nurse. Eventually, it was the children who at first waved and then spoke to me.

It became obvious that although the reserves were just across the road from one another, they were run in completely different ways. On one reserve, I shared an office with one other person. From the start, she let me know that she did not like to share her space. Frequently, I would arrive on a Tuesday morning to find all my papers and other things I had left on my desk on the floor. It was also a problem when I needed to see a patient, especially when a baby's vaccine was due. This lasted for some time, but after talking many times to the band manager and others, an apartment was rented on reserve land, away from the band office. This I had to also share, but it had a living room, a kitchen and one bedroom in which I was able to set up my office and clinic space.

Problems arose on the days other groups were using the living room, and I was told not to disturb them. On at least two occasions, if they forgot to tell me they were coming and I had to get out and get my work done, I had to climb out of the window. I was in that apartment for several months, but eventually another apartment was found in the same complex. This time, it had three bedrooms, giving me space and others room for groups and events.

On the other reserve, I shared a space in the band office with the rest of the staff. No room was provided, but I had a desk upstairs that I had to share. I set up a tiny clinic room downstairs, near the reception desk. When a baby had a vaccine, the whole staff was made aware since crying and screaming often ensued. Eventually, a trailer was brought in and set up. I moved in and had a room of my own. Other people also had rooms, and over time a daycare was set up in the biggest area. This worked well for everybody, and we were able to coordinate some of our events. The third move occurred in my forth year when a new band office was built. It was situated next to the Big House, where all the ceremonial activities took place, and was much bigger than the old band office. There was quite a celebration when it finally opened. All permanent staff had their own office, with the nurse's office near the front door. There was also a good-sized reception area and a kitchen.

I worked two days on Songhees, the bigger community and one day on Esquimalt. It was not nearly enough time to get the work done, so it was essential to prioritize tasks. All the usual public health duties were undertaken, which included clinics and home visits, and after a long time, I was more accepted and got into a routine. I did realize fairly quickly that all mail was opened by the receptionists. Because much of the information in my mail was of a private nature, I made arrangements to have any results of medical tests sent to the provincial public health office in the town of Esquimalt. I went there every Tuesday, on my way to work, to pick up my mail, have time to speak to other nurses, and catch up on any new events.

Into the Unknown

View from one of my communities. The Reserves were mostly surrounded by buildings; however there were places where a more natural view was possible.

As I was increasingly accepted and trusted by the band members in the reserves, home visits became easier, and more mothers and babies came for their vaccines. The Esquimalt

Neighbourhood House group had been coming to both reserves to provide a lunch and talk to people about various topics. I continued this event, developing it into a Best Babies group where over lunch we discussed topics of interest to young mothers and the occasional father. Sometimes we made crafts for certain celebrations, like Easter and Christmas.

Eventually, the Neighbourhood House dropped their involvement with the communities, so I — with the help of a couple of the mothers — started providing lunch. We cooked in my office kitchen in one reserve and eventually used the kitchen in someone's home, on the other. These twice monthly gatherings were well attended, and we enjoyed our basic meal together, as well as the discussions that followed.

My first invitation to the Big House, an important building in which ceremonies are conducted and various community gatherings take place, was unfortunately a funeral. I was warned beforehand not to discuss anything that I saw there, outside the building. This I never did, despite attending many functions and ceremonies over the years. I often volunteered to help out in the kitchen when an event was to take place. It was a great way to have time to speak to the other helpers and for them to get to know me.

I was once asked to see a boy who was living in the Big House while being introduced to tradition and ceremony. I was blindfolded and led to his area inside before having the blindfold removed to enable me to examine the patient. This never happened any of the other times I was in Big House, so must have been the choice of the official at the time.

Over the years, I went to several funerals, many graduation ceremonies, and naming ceremonies. Once, I attended a special dance rite where I was the only non-Indigenous person present. I learned quickly to sit quietly and just observe when I was in the Big House. I was allowed to participate in a burning ceremony, once, where, as a part of the activities, a plate of special food is offered to the fire. I offered a plate for my father who had died a few years earlier.

A member of Songhees Nation organized two powwows. Many people from all over came to enjoy these weekends. They were great occasions, with lots of stalls where art, crafts, and food could be purchased. Dancing competitions took place with all the competitors in their distinctive regalia. Once the official dancing ended, people from the audience were invited to join in a Round Dance where all participants danced, to the beat of the drums, round in a huge circle.

On Songhees reserve, a food bank was set up in a small room in the basement of a former school. One band member took charge and organized the procurement of the food and the running of the facility. She and I worked together to regularly check the stock and find recipes. When a more unusual ingredient came in, we found ideas on how to cook it.

We had a health fair one weekend, where health information was given out and cultural events took place. The Best Babies group had, for weeks in advance, collected the large tins that coffee comes in. These we filled with small items that would be useful if a disaster occurred, such as an earthquake. They became a sought-after item which we sold at a reasonable price to offset the cost.

I wrote a regular monthly newsletter to circulate in one of the communities. This allowed me to give new information about health matters on a regular basis. At first, people in the band office were not too sure about this new publication. In the end, it not only became a health information paper, but was used to give other information about band events.

I had previously participated in the World Friendship Walk, which was a 5k event taking place in various cities throughout the world. It was an easy walk, where meeting people from many nationalities was the main activity. I put out the idea of the walk to a few people from the community and was pleased when nine agreed to join me. The next time the same walk came again to the area, we met again, with several more participants this time.

At one time in Songhees reserve, we had three ladies with breast cancer. To give them encouragement, many family members, people in the community and I, did the 5k walk for Breast Cancer. The money we raised went to cancer research.

Many of us in the other community participated in the Times Colonist 10k. This annual event takes place around the centre of Victoria and attracts runners and walkers from all over. A group of us participated and were regarded afterwards by band members' as achieving quite an accomplishment, with photographs of the participants hanging in the band office, boosting the feeling of success.

We had great Christmas parties in both communities. In one, the whole community got together about a week before Christmas for a full Christmas dinner with turkey and all the trimmings. Every child received a present from Santa. In the other, the dinner was for elders, and each of them received a small gift.

The staff of both communities also got together at Christmas time for lunch, which the bands paid for, at various restaurants in Victoria and I was fortunate to be invited to these occasions. Our employer, ITHA, also had a Christmas party for staff in Nanaimo where we all received a gift, which was sometimes something useful like a fire extinguisher, but at other times a more personal item.

I enjoyed visiting many elders who gave me insights into their history and the history of the nation. Many had attended residential schools and had stories to tell about their treatment there. Some who had attended continued to belong to the Catholic Church, but most did not. The Shaker Church became a more prominent church to which many people belonged and participated in. I am not aware of how it got the name Shaker, but the services are conducted on Indigenous ceremony. Often at a funeral, it was the Shaker congregation that conducted the service.

New houses were built on both reserves, giving much needed accommodation for families who were often living in overcrowded conditions. Though the overcrowding continued, no family member was turned away if they needed a bed for the night.

***

My time with ITHA had its ups and downs, but on the whole I enjoyed the work. Eventually, there were difficulties at its headquarters. Luckily, the nursing department was only aware of the rumours, and we continued with our work in relative isolation. Gradually, the whole department deteriorated and I decided, despite originally planning to retire at sixty-five, to follow a dream to go to art school. I therefore put in my notice early, at aged sixty two, applied, and was accepted in the diploma program at the local art school.

Both the reserves and the ITHA gave me great send-offs. Gifts were presented during our meals together. I would not have missed the experience of working on the reserves, despite the poor start. I keep in touch with many members of the two communities by phone or the internet, on a regular basis, and I often meet band members at events.

Eventually, the ITHA completely collapsed, and another health group took over. The nurses I knew all scattered in various directions, and I hear about them on rare occasions.

Summary

After forty-three years in nursing, with thirty-five of those years as a public health nurse, I had to think long and hard before deciding to retire earlier than first intended. I enjoyed the work most of the time, despite all the ups and downs. My experiences gave me confidence to try new ways of working, and if they did not work, I felt secure enough to let them drop and try another way.

I was accepted, on the whole, in the many communities I worked in and had been given the privilege of attending many cultural events. I travelled from coast to coast experiencing a vast array of lifestyles and beliefs. Working in and for communities allows for a very different view and insight into how other people live.

In high school, I had done a higher level in art and dreamt of going to art school. My art teacher discouraged me from even trying when he told me I could draw and paint, but not well enough. This pushed me in another, very different, direction, which I have not regretted. The dream was still something I thought about, even after all those years, and retirement would give me time to concentrate on art and prove to myself that I was capable.

I checked my bank account, calculated my expenses, and although my pension was going to be small, I knew I could pull it off. On my first week of retirement, I went to the local art school and talked to the director. She said I should apply. I wrote and submitted my admission paper and portfolio. I heard fairly quickly that I could start. I took classes at the school part time initially then switched to full time in my final year. Eventually, I gained a diploma in Fine Art.

In my retirement years, I have continued to paint, lawn bowl, sing, and walk daily. I have travelled to many exciting countries, meeting small groups of people on adventure tours. This kind of travel has given me the opportunity to explore places — by various travel means — that many tourists miss if they just go on a bus tour or a cruise. I have thoroughly enjoyed Peru, Ecuador, India, and Cuba on some of these trips. I continue to have travel plans and intend to keep stepping into the unknown for as long as I am able.

Printed in Canada